Sweet Simplicity

Jacques Pépin's
Fruit Desserts

Jacques Pépin

Principal Photography by Penina

Additional Photography by Tim Turner

Design by Madeleine Corson Design

Illustrations by Jacques Pépin

Bay Books

San Francisco

"A FAITHFUL FRIEND IS THE MEDICINE OF LIFE."
TO MY BEST FRIEND AND *PÂTISSIER EXTRAORDINAIRE*, JEAN-CLAUDE,
I DEDICATE THIS BOOK OF "SWEET FRIENDSHIP."

BAY BOOKS IS AN IMPRINT OF BAY BOOKS & TAPES, INC.,
555 DE HARO STREET, SUITE 220, SAN FRANCISCO, CA 94107.

MANAGING EDITOR: ZIPPORAH W. COLLINS

BOOK DESIGNER: MADELEINE CORSON DESIGN

COPYEDITOR: ZIPPORAH W. COLLINS

PROOFREADERS: DESNE BORDER, KAREN STOUGH

INDEXER: ELINOR LINDHEIMER

ILLUSTRATOR: JACQUES PÉPIN

PHOTOGRAPHERS: PENINA, TIM TURNER

PHOTOGRAPHY COORDINATORS: VINCENT NATTRESS, TINA SALTER

PROP STYLISTS: HEIDI GINTNER, CAROL HACKER, SARA SLAVIN

FOOD STYLISTS: POUKÉ, BERNIE SHIMBKE

ASSISTANT STYLIST: LORRAINE BATTLE

PHOTOGRAPHY CHEFS: CARL ABBOTT, LAURA AMMONS, GARY DANKO,
JACK ERVIN, ROBERT LEWIS, BRIAN MILLER, VINCENT NATTRESS

ASSISTANTS TO JACQUES PÉPIN: NORMA GALEHOUSE, TINA SALTER

NUTRITIONAL CONSULTANTS: HILL NUTRITION, LAURA PENSIERO

THE PUBLISHER WISHES TO THANK PAULA LINTON OF GREENLEAF PRODUCE,
AND SUR LA TABLE FOR FOOD AND PROP ASSISTANCE.

LIBRARY OF CONGRESS CATALOGING-IN-PUBLICATION DATA AVAILABLE

PRINTED IN CHINA

10 9 8 7 6 5 4 3 2 1

DISTRIBUTED BY PUBLISHERS GROUP WEST

CONTENTS

E V E R Y D A Y M E A L S do not usually include dessert at my house. Desserts are generally added when we have dinner or weekend guests. However, the exception is fruit.

Where would desserts be without fruit? It is the most useful, plentiful, and eclectic of all ingredients in the dessert pantry. Without fruit, we wouldn't have fruit juices, preserves, jams, or chutneys. We wouldn't have fruit flavorings for mousse, and there would be almost no toppings for tarts, no purees for sherbets and ices. Most soft drinks would disappear from the market, and we would have no orange juice to start our days.

I still enjoy following the seasons with fruit, relishing early spring strawberries and rhubarb, delighting in all of the summer berries, looking forward to apples and pears in the fall, and welcoming bananas, pineapples, and oranges in the winter. More and more, however, the traditional lines dividing fruits by season have been crossed by markets throughout the country, so that a great many fruits that our parents consumed only at a given time of year are now available year-round. This is good; it gives the cook more choices throughout the year. Furthermore, fruits that years ago were somewhat esoteric and expensive are now plentiful and, generally, reasonably priced. I remember as a child eating oranges and pineapples from Algeria; these ordinary choices in today's markets were then somewhat exotic and not readily available to our family. The variety of fruits offered at any supermarket in the United States is now staggering, and every year more fruits—Asian, exotic, tropical, and new hybrids—are added. The quality varies from fair to very good, and the prices are amazingly low for most of the fruits.

Still, one cannot overemphasize that ripeness and quality determine whether a fruit dessert will be extraordinary or merely ordinary. Nothing can match freshly picked cherries or apricots. Ripened on the tree, cherries are bursting with juicy berry flavor and apricots are soft and sweet, with a creamy, golden-orange interior. Often, unfortunately, fruits at the market fall short of this tree-ripened standard. Then the knowledge of the cook comes into play in substituting a better-quality fruit and changing the recipe to accommodate it.

Seasons are still important. Even though raspberries and strawberries are usually available all year, I can hardly wait until summer, when I can go to a farm and pick berries that are fully ripened on the vine. It's great fun, the price is good, and the fruit is at its peak of maturity, quality, and nutrition. While strawberries or raspberries at a local market in January can fool your eyes, your palate will not be fooled. Now, there are times, even in full winter, when good-quality fruit is available, depending on where it comes from. Finding it is a trial-and-error process. Be critical in choosing your fruits. To determine whether a melon, for example, is sweet, smell the stem end; a ripe, good-quality melon will have a delicate melon aroma. If the fruit isn't up to par, select a different fruit that is high in quality, or make a different dessert.

Soil, weather, and climate affect where specific fruits grow best, and it is always beneficial to investigate farms or growers near to where you live and try to get fresh fruits from regional sources. It is also important to voice concern about the practice of spraying insecticides, fungicides, and other additives on fruit; the more natural a fruit is, the better it is for our health.

Some fruits are more reliably good and easier to work with than others. Oranges and other citrus fruits are quite reliable year-round. In the fall, the range of apples and pears is so abundant that there is always one variety at its peak that will work in whatever recipe you are preparing.

This book features well over a hundred recipes for desserts made with fruit. Still, if you don't have time to prepare the recipes, remember that ripe, high-quality fruits can always be enjoyed *au naturel,* eaten plain, which is usually the way we consume fruits in my family. When guests come to dine, however, the peaches we ordinarily eat right from the bowl might be transformed into a peach Melba, consisting of a poached peach and a raspberry puree, served with a little ice cream.

Fruit desserts are the most symphonic of all desserts. As the culmination of a meal or its grand finale, fruit brings flavors together, cleans your palate, is generally low in calories and low in fat, is conducive to digestion, and does not weigh heavily on your stomach. A fruit dessert makes it easy to comply with the USDA recommendation of five servings daily from the vegetable/fruit food group. For those who are interested in nutritive content, I provide a nutritional analysis of each dessert with the recipe. (The analyses do not include optional ingredients.)

Not many foods from large supermarkets are as dependable as fruits. They are graded and selected by distributors according to very strict rules, with the cooperation of the market and the grower, and they are controlled by state regulations. There is no better snack than an orange, apple, or banana and no better breakfast starter than orange or grapefruit juice. It is refreshing to start a meal with a fruit salad and end it with a roasted pear or a raspberry sherbet. If you are lucky enough to live in a good growing area and to have a house with a garden (or an orchard), then you know that nothing can duplicate the pleasure of picking your own fruit off the tree or vine, whether you eat it right on the spot or transform it into a wonderful dessert in your kitchen.

When you prepare the recipes in this book, remember to consider the quality of the fruit, and don't hesitate to substitute one fruit for another if the specified fruit is not available in your area or if the quality is not what it should be. You can create many additional recipes from those I offer here, with a little imagination. Use the same techniques, from poaching to making a puree or sauce, but substitute different fruits and use different combinations, different colors, and different textures to develop your own desserts.

In *The Concise Encyclopedia of Gastronomy* (1952), André Simon eulogizes fruit: "Fruit is the womb that holds, protects, feeds, matures and eventually delivers the seed responsible for the survival of the species and its propagation. Night and day the roots distill from the moist earth and their leaves distill from the moist air the food and drink which tree, bush, herb or plant needs, not merely to live but also and chiefly to bring forth a living seed."

Fruit is suitable for all occasions and is an important part of all cuisines, all cooking styles. It is good for children, for old people, for everyone, for family meals as well as formal dinners. When you're indecisive about what kind of dessert to make for a party, go with a fruit dessert. It is most likely to succeed, as virtually no one refuses such a treat. Happy cooking!

Jacques Pépin

APPLES

Apples are the fruit eaten most often in the United States. Red and Golden Delicious apples are the most popular of the more than five thousand species that have been identified for at least three thousand years. About a hundred apple varieties are grown commercially in the United States, with an annual production of about 180 million bushels. Washington State produces the most, although the Northeast, from New York to Maine, and California are also great producers. ✎ Apple varieties have an extraordinary range of tastes, from very simple and straightforward to very lemony to more complex tastes resembling banana and strawberry. Textures range from crisp to soft. Sizes vary as well; large apples can weigh as much as half a pound. ✎ Cooking apples are often distinguished from eating apples based on their texture. Generally, green apples, such as Granny Smith, pippin, and Golden Delicious, are considered cooking apples. The Golden Delicious, which may be greenish yellow or all yellow, depending on ripeness, has a creamy texture, retains its shape when cooked, and is, to me, the best all-around apple. The russet is well known in France as a *reinette du Canada*. This variety gets its name from the dots of darker color on its skin, which some people find objectionable, but these weather marks do not hurt the quality of

Freshly harvested apples will keep in a cool cellar for the whole winter, although their skins may shrivel a little.

the apple. For me, the russet is one of the best for juice and flesh. The Rome Beauty,

Stayman, McIntosh, Jonathan, and Empire are all white-fleshed, with a soft texture that

makes them good for sauces or dishes in which the cooked apples need not hold their shape.

They have a lemony taste, and some also have a slight banana flavor. ✐ When ripe, apples

will be firm and crisp to the touch, not soft. Stored in a brown bag, apples release ethylene

gas, which induces ripening. (This also works with underripe vegetables, including green

tomatoes.) ✐ Apples are not only good for desserts but also excellent sautéed as a side

dish with rich meats or poultry, such as pork, goose, or duck. Normandy, in northwestern

France, produces a sparkling cider from apples in the style of champagne. I enjoy making

this sparkling wine at home with New England apples, and I think the result as good as the

Normandy version. ✐ Although apples are available year-round, they are best in late fall

when picked right off the tree. Choose apples with a bright color and a smooth skin. ✐

Myths about apples range from Newton discovering the law of gravity with an apple to

William Tell shooting an apple off his son's head to Greek and Roman references to a loved

one as "the apple of one's eye."

"An apple a day keeps the doctor away" may indeed be true; apples are high in vitamins A and C and very rich in fiber.

SWEET APPLE FLAKE CONFECTIONS

When dried in a convection oven, thin, unpeeled apple slices are transformed into crisp flakes with a flavor I find almost addictive. Pressed into scoops of frozen yogurt, as they are in this recipe, the flakes are a delicious substitute for cookies. They also make a great, healthful snack on their own and can be served as a garnish for custard or ice cream.

1   *firm apple (8 ounces), preferably Golden Delicious, russet, or Rome Beauty*
1   *pint low-fat vanilla or coffee frozen yogurt*

1. Preheat a convection oven to 250 degrees.

2. Using a sharp, thin-bladed or serrated knife, cut the unpeeled apple crosswise into slices ⅛ inch thick. You should have about sixteen slices. If desired, remove the pits from the center slices. Arrange the slices in one layer, side by side, on an aluminum cookie sheet.

3. Place the cookie sheet in the oven, and cook the apple slices for about 1 hour, or until they are fairly dry and very lightly browned. Remove the slices from the sheet while they are still warm and flexible, and arrange them on a platter. Cool them to room temperature. The flakes should then be dry and crunchy. Place them in a metal or plastic storage container with a tight lid, and store them at room temperature until ready to use.

4. About 1½ to 2 hours before serving time, transfer the frozen yogurt from the freezer to the refrigerator to soften.

5. At serving time, place a large scoop of frozen yogurt in the center of each of four dessert plates. Press four of the apple flakes around the sides and across the top of each scoop, encasing the scoop with the apples. (Or, arrange the apple flakes on or around the yogurt scoops in another design to your liking.) Serve immediately.

YIELD

4 servings

TOTAL TIME

1½ to 2 hours

NUTRITIONAL ANALYSIS PER SERVING

Calories 131

Protein 4 g

Carbohydrates 26 g

Fat 1 g

Saturated fat 0 g

Cholesterol 5 mg

Sodium 55 mg

CHEESE, APPLE, AND NUT MÉLANGE

The combination of flavors here—cheese, nuts, and apples that have been rolled in lemon juice and sprinkled with black pepper—is delicious. Although I usually serve the mélange as a dessert, it also makes an ideal brunch or light lunch main dish. To crush whole peppercorns coarsely (creating what the French call a *mignonette*), spread them on a clean, flat work surface, and press on them with the base of a saucepan until they crack open. Pepper crushed this way is much less hot than pepper ground conventionally. If you must use a pepper mill, however, set it to grind the pepper as coarsely as possible.

YIELD

4 servings

TOTAL TIME

About 15 minutes

NUTRITIONAL ANALYSIS PER SERVING

Calories 303

Protein 10 g

Carbohydrates 18 g

Fat 23 g

Saturated fat 8 g

Cholesterol 27 mg

Sodium 511 mg

2   *large apples (russet, Golden Delicious, or Rome Beauty)*

2   *tablespoons lemon juice*

½   *teaspoon black peppercorns, coarsely crushed (see introduction, above)*

⅔   *cup pecans (about 25 halves)*

5   *ounces blue cheese (Gorgonzola, Stilton, or Roquefort), cut into 4 pieces*

4   *sprigs basil or arugula (about 5 ounces)*
    French bread

1. Preheat the oven to 375 degrees.

2. Cut the unpeeled apples into quarters, remove and discard the cores, and roll the quarters in the lemon juice. Sprinkle the apples with the pepper.

3. Spread the pecans on a cookie sheet, and bake them for 8 minutes.

4. To serve, arrange two pieces of apple, one piece of cheese, and a few pecans on each of four plates. Arrange a few basil leaves or arugula sprigs around the apples. Serve with crusty French bread.

Cheese, Apple, and Nut Mélange (this page).

SPICY APPLE CHARLOTTE

I use russet apples here, but another variety can be substituted. The apples are cooked on top of the stove initially in a flavorful mixture of sugar, honey, and spices. Then, when most of the moisture has evaporated and the apple slices are brown, they are baked between layers of bread in a cake pan. The unmolded charlotte is coated with a peach jam mixture and served in slices, warm or at room temperature, with a spoonful of sour cream or plain yogurt, if desired.

YIELD

6 to 8 servings

TOTAL TIME

About 1¼ hours

NUTRITIONAL ANALYSIS PER SERVING (8 SERVINGS)

Calories 260

Protein 2 g

Carbohydrates 52 g

Fat 6 g

Saturated fat 2 g

Cholesterol 5 mg

Sodium 146 mg

1   tablespoon unsalted butter

1½ tablespoons corn oil or safflower oil

2   pounds russet apples (about 5), peeled, cored, and cut into ¼-inch slices

¼   cup sugar

¼   cup honey

1   teaspoon ground cinnamon

¼   teaspoon ground allspice

⅛   teaspoon ground cloves

9   very thin slices fine-textured white bread (6½ ounces)

3   tablespoons strained peach jam

1½ teaspoons calvados (apple brandy) (optional) or lemon juice, orange juice, or water

Sour cream or plain yogurt (optional)

1. Preheat the oven to 375 degrees.

2. Heat the butter and 1 tablespoon of the oil in a large saucepan. When they are hot, add the apples, and sauté them for 1 minute. Then add the sugar, honey, cinnamon, allspice, and cloves, mix gently, cover, and cook over medium heat for 10 minutes. Most of the moisture from the apples should be gone at this point; remove the lid, and cook the apples, uncovered, for 5 to 6 minutes, or until they are nicely browned.

3. Using the remaining ½ tablespoon of oil, oil a round cake pan 8 inches in diameter and 1½ inches deep.

4. Trim and reserve the crusts from the nine slices of bread. Cut four of the slices in half lengthwise to make eight rectangles, each 3 by 1½ inches, and arrange these rectangles so they fit snugly around the sides of the oiled pan. Cut the remaining five slices of bread in half diagonally to create ten triangles. Arrange these triangles so they completely cover the bottom of the pan.

5. Spoon the apple mixture on top of the bread in the pan, and spread it evenly into the corners of the pan. Smooth the surface, then crumble the reserved bread trimmings on top of the apples so that most of them are covered.

6. Bake the charlotte for 20 to 25 minutes. Meanwhile, in a small bowl, combine the strained peach jam with the calvados, if desired, or lemon juice, orange juice, or water.

7. Let the charlotte cool on a rack for 10 minutes, then invert it onto a plate. No more than 20 to 30 minutes before serving, coat the surface of the dessert with the peach mixture. (If the coating is applied earlier, it will be absorbed by the dessert.)

8. Cut the charlotte into wedges, and top each serving with a dollop of sour cream or yogurt, if desired.

MÉMÉ'S APPLE TART

I remember well the famous apple tart my mother made every day as a dessert offering in her small Lyon restaurant, Le Pélican. Her dough was unlike any other; its tender, crumbly, airy texture was created by combining vegetable shortening, baking powder, and warm milk with the flour. I hope you enjoy this taste I associate with memories from my youth.

YIELD

6 to 8 servings

TOTAL TIME

About 1½ hours, plus cooling time

—

NUTRITIONAL ANALYSIS PER SERVING (8 SERVINGS)

Calories 299

Protein 3 g

Carbohydrates 40 g

Fat 15 g

Saturated fat 5 g

Cholesterol 10 mg

Sodium 79 mg

DOUGH

1¼ cups all-purpose flour
1 teaspoon sugar
½ teaspoon baking powder
⅛ teaspoon salt
6 tablespoons hydrogenated vegetable shortening (such as Crisco)
¼ cup milk, heated to lukewarm

FILLING

2 pounds McIntosh apples (6 medium)
3 tablespoons sugar
2 tablespoons unsalted butter

FOR THE DOUGH

1. Preheat the oven to 400 degrees.

2. Combine the flour, sugar, baking powder, and salt in a bowl. Add the shortening, and mix with a spoon or with your hands until the mixture feels and looks sandy. Add the warm milk, and mix rapidly until the dough forms into a ball.

3. Roll out the ball of dough between two sheets of plastic wrap to form a circle 11 to 12 inches in diameter, then remove the top sheet, and invert the dough into a 9-inch tart or quiche pan with a removable bottom. Use the remaining plastic sheet to gently press the dough into the pan. Remove any dough overhang by running your rolling pin across the top edge of the pan.

FOR THE FILLING

4. Peel the apples, quarter them, and remove the cores. Arrange the apple quarters on top of the dough, and sprinkle the sugar evenly over them. Cut the butter into small pieces, and dot the apples with them.

5. Place the tart on a cookie sheet, and bake it for 1 hour. Cool the tart to lukewarm, cut it into wedges, and serve.

APPLES GRANDMA

This classic French-style apple dessert is made with whole, cored, unpeeled apples. In this recipe, I place slices of bread underneath the apples. The slices soak up the juice of the apples, the apricot preserves, and the grenadine to produce a very flavorful dessert, especially when it is served lukewarm.

4   Golden Delicious apples (about 2 pounds)
4   thin slices bread (2 ounces)
5   sprigs fresh mint
1½ tablespoons unsalted butter
¼   cup apricot preserves
2   tablespoons grenadine syrup
½   cup water
2   tablespoons sugar
3   tablespoons pine nuts

Apples Grandma (this page).

1. Preheat the oven to 400 degrees.

2. Core the apples, and peel the skin from the top third of each apple.

3. Arrange the four slices of bread in a single layer in a gratin dish, and place an apple, peeled side up, in the center of each slice. Place a sprig of mint in the hole in the center of each apple, then divide the butter among the apples, placing it on top of the mint in each hole.

4. In a small bowl, mix together the apricot preserves, grenadine, and water. Pour the mixture over the apples, and sprinkle them with the sugar and nuts.

5. Bake the apples for 1 to 1¼ hours, or until the apples are very tender and nicely browned on top. Cool the dessert to lukewarm or room temperature, garnish it with the remaining mint sprig, and serve one apple per person with some of the nuts and surrounding juices.

YIELD
4 servings

TOTAL TIME
About 1½ hours, plus cooling time

NUTRITIONAL ANALYSIS PER SERVING
Calories 337
Protein 4 g
Carbohydrates 65 g
Fat 9 g
Saturated fat 3 g
Cholesterol 12 mg
Sodium 90 mg

APPLE ROUNDS WITH CALVADOS GLAZE

A new twist on the classic apple tart, these individual desserts consist of apple slices baked on large circles of dough. Served with a strategically arranged "stem" and some "leaves" of cooked dough alongside, each finished dessert resembles an apple. A glaze of apricot preserves mixed with a little calvados intensifies the flavor of the apples and gives them a polished look.

DOUGH

¾ *cup all-purpose flour (4 ounces)*
½ *stick unsalted butter (2 ounces),
    cut while frozen into ½-inch-thick slices*
1 *teaspoon sugar*
1 *small pinch salt*
2 *tablespoons cold water*

GARNISH

2 *Golden Delicious apples (about
    14 ounces total)*
1 *tablespoon sugar*

GLAZE

3 *tablespoons excellent-quality
    apricot preserves*
2 *teaspoons calvados (apple brandy) or,
    if unavailable, cognac*

FOR THE DOUGH

1. Place the flour, frozen butter pieces, 1 teaspoon of sugar, and salt in the bowl of a food processor. Process for 5 to 10 seconds, or just until the mixture looks granulated. Add the cold water, and process for another 5 seconds. (The mixture will not have gathered together yet.) Transfer the mixture to a piece of plastic wrap, and press it together into a ball.

2. Roll out the ball of dough between two sheets of plastic wrap until it is very thin (about ⅛ inch) and measures about 8 by 10 inches. Using a cookie cutter about 4 inches in diameter, cut out four circles of dough. Line a cookie sheet with a nonstick baking mat or parchment paper, and place the dough circles on it.

3. With the leftover dough, cut eight oval shapes to make "leaves," each about 2½ inches long and 1½ inches wide. Mark the leaves with the dull edge of a knife blade to imitate the veins of a leaf. Make apple "stems" by rolling four small pieces of dough to form cylinders or sticks, each about ¼ inch thick and 2 inches long. Place these stems and leaves on the cookie sheet with the dough circles. (You can use any leftover dough to make a free-form cookie to eat at your leisure, and place it on the cookie sheet with the other dough shapes.)

4. Preheat the oven to 400 degrees.

FOR THE GARNISH

5. Peel the apples, and core them whole with a sharp knife, apple corer, or vegetable peeler. Cut each apple crosswise into twelve thin slices. Place six slices on each dough circle, arranging the larger slices on the bottoms of the circles and the remaining ones overlapping in a circular manner on top, and finishing with the smallest slice in the center. Alternatively, cut the peeled, cored apples into thin wedges, and arrange the wedges, overlapping slightly, in a concentric pattern on top of the dough circles. Sprinkle the apples with the 1 tablespoon of sugar, dividing it among the four desserts.

6. Place the cookie sheet in the preheated oven, and bake for about 20 minutes. Remove the leaves carefully with a spatula, and arrange them on a rack to cool. Return the cookie sheet to the oven for about 10 minutes more, and then remove the stems. Continue baking the apple tartlets for about 20 minutes more (a total of 50 minutes), or until the apples are nicely browned and the dough underneath them is very crisp. Place the tartlets on a cooling rack until luke-warm, then arrange them on four individual dessert plates.

FOR THE GLAZE

7. Mix the preserves and calvados together in a small bowl, and coat the top of each warm tartlet with the mixture, applying it carefully with a pastry brush or spoon.

8. Arrange the pastry leaves and stems alongside each tartlet to make it resemble an apple. Serve the desserts immediately.

BAKED APPLE TART

In this dish, cored, halved apples filled with apricot jam are baked in a round of pastry dough. ◠ The classic dough for this dessert is suitable for most baking needs and is easily made in a food processor. It is important that you not overmix the dough ingredients. The butter should not be totally incorporated into the flour; visible pieces will melt as the dough cooks, and it will develop some of the flakiness of puff pastry.

DOUGH

3 tablespoons unsalted butter
¾ cup all-purpose flour (3 ounces)
½ teaspoon sugar
2 tablespoons ice water

FILLING

2 large Golden Delicious apples (1 pound)
2 tablespoons apricot jam
1 tablespoon sugar
½ tablespoon unsalted butter

FOR THE DOUGH

1. Preheat the oven to 400 degrees.

2. Cut the 3 tablespoons of butter into ½-inch pieces. Place the flour, butter pieces, and ½ teaspoon sugar in the bowl of a food processor. Process for 5 seconds, add the water, and process for another 5 seconds. Remove the dough, even if it is not compactly mixed, then press it and roll it out between two layers of plastic wrap to form a circle about 10 inches in diameter. Remove the top layer of wrap, and invert the dough onto a cookie sheet. Peel off the remaining wrap, and refrigerate the dough.

FOR THE FILLING

3. Meanwhile, peel the apples, cut them in half, and remove the cores. Hollow the apples out a little with a measuring spoon, and chop the trimmings. (You should have about ¾ cup.) Place ½ tablespoon of the jam in the hollow of each apple half, and arrange the halves, filled side down, in the center of the circle of dough. Sprinkle the chopped apple around the halves.

4. Bring the edges of the dough up over the apples to create a border, 1 to 2 inches high, all around. (This will hold the cooking juices inside.)

5. Sprinkle the top of the tart with the 1 tablespoon of sugar, and dot with the ½ tablespoon of butter. Bake for 45 to 60 minutes, until well browned. Serve warm or at room temperature.

Top: Caramelized Apple Timbales (see page 22); bottom: Baked Apple Tart (this page).

YIELD
4 servings

TOTAL TIME
About 1½ hours

**NUTRITIONAL
ANALYSIS
PER SERVING**
Calories 260
Protein 3 g
Carbohydrates 41 g
Fat 11 g
Saturated fat 6 g
Cholesterol 27 mg
Sodium 6 mg

CARAMELIZED APPLE TIMBALES

This dessert is a fine choice for a dinner party, because it can be made ahead. Line the tiny soufflé molds with plastic wrap before arranging the cooked, caramelized apples inside, so the timbales are easy to unmold. I don't peel the apples; I enjoy the chewiness and texture that the skin gives to the dish. The concentrated apple–caramel taste is particularly pleasing when the timbales are served with a little sour cream or yogurt. (See photograph, page 20.)

YIELD
4 servings

TOTAL TIME
About 45 minutes,
plus cooling time

———

NUTRITIONAL ANALYSIS PER SERVING
Calories 199
Protein 1 g
Carbohydrates 38 g
Fat 7 g
Saturated fat 4 g
Cholesterol 14 mg
Sodium 10 mg

4 *large Golden Delicious apples (about 1½ pounds)*
2 *tablespoons lemon juice*
¼ *cup sugar*
3 *tablespoons water*
2 *teaspoons julienned lemon rind*
⅓ *cup water*
1 *tablespoon unsalted butter*
4 *tablespoons sour cream or plain yogurt*

1. Remove the apple stems together with a little of the adjoining skin and flesh. Place the stems in a bowl with the lemon juice, and set them aside for use as a decoration.

2. Cut the apples in half lengthwise, and core them. Then cut each half crosswise into ¼-inch-thick slices to make about 6 loosely packed cups.

3. In a skillet, combine the sugar and the 3 tablespoons of water, and cook over medium-high heat until the mixture becomes a dark brown caramel (3 to 4 minutes). Add the apple slices, the lemon rind, the ⅓ cup of water, and the butter. Mix well, cover, reduce the heat to low, and cook at a gentle boil for about 7 minutes, or until the apples are tender and most of the moisture is gone. Remove the lid, and cook for about 5 minutes over high heat, rolling the apples in the sauce, until the sauce has turned into caramel again and the apple pieces are browned. Let cool to lukewarm.

4. Meanwhile, line four small soufflé molds or ramekins (½- to ¾-cup capacity) with plastic wrap. Pack the lukewarm apple mixture into the molds, cover the molds with plastic wrap, and refrigerate them until cold.

5. At serving time, unmold the timbales, and decorate them with the reserved apple stems. Serve each with a tablespoon of sour cream or yogurt.

GRATIN OF APPLES, WALNUTS, AND GRANOLA

This recipe couldn't be easier. No need to peel the apples; just cut them into chunks, combine them with the granola, walnuts, and orange juice, press the mixture into a gratin dish, and bake. The final product is delicious served with a little sour cream, whipped cream, or even nonfat plain yogurt.

2 apples (preferably russet or Opalescent)
1 cup low-fat granola mixture
¼ cup walnut pieces
2 tablespoons sugar
¼ cup orange juice
4 tablespoons sour cream or whipped cream for garnish (optional)

1. Preheat the oven to 400 degrees.

2. Cut the apples in half, core them, and cut them into 1-inch cubes. (You should have about 4 cups.)

3. In a bowl, thoroughly mix the apple cubes with the granola, walnuts, sugar, and orange juice, and press the mixture lightly into a 6-cup gratin dish. Bake for 1 hour, or until the apples are soft and the dessert is nicely browned on top.

4. Serve lukewarm or at room temperature, topping each serving with 1 tablespoon of sour cream or whipped cream, if desired.

YIELD
4 servings

TOTAL TIME
About 1½ hours, plus cooling time

———

NUTRITIONAL ANALYSIS PER SERVING
Calories 202
Protein 3 g
Carbohydrates 38 g
Fat 6 g
Saturated fat 1 g
Cholesterol 0 mg
Sodium 32 mg

APRICOTS

O f all the fruits, apricots have the fondest memories for me. Their deep yellow-orange flesh, slightly elastic and soft, made the best jam I've ever tasted. I still make apricot jam when I am fortunate enough to get overripe apricots right from the tree at a nearby farm. Misshapen apricots with dark spots make great desserts and jam. The quality and ripeness of the fruit determine whether the dessert will be ordinary or sublime.

Apricots have been cultivated for more than three thousand years, and the most prolific crops in the United States come from California, where apricots were first grown in the eighteenth century. A *Prunus* genus relative of the almond and the peach (as well as the nectarine, plum, and cherry), the apricot has an intense flavor. The most common varieties are the Royal and the Tilton. Apricots should be picked when plump and ripe and are usually available fresh from May to August. In older fruit, the skin shrivels and becomes deeper in color, and the flesh becomes softer in texture. Canned and dried apricots are available year-round. Canned apricots can be excellent if used properly. The best dried apricots, in my opinion, come from California and Turkey. Dried apricots are usually treated with sulfur dioxide to retain their beautiful color. Untreated, they turn

For me, no apricots can compare to those of the Rhône Valley that I picked as a child with my godfather, who worked in an abundant fruit orchard.

almost brown, but their taste is still fine. ☙ I usually keep apricots in a fruit bowl on the table and consume them before they go bad. They continue ripening a little at room temperature. When they are really ripe, I put them in a plastic bag and refrigerate them. They will keep this way for a few days but will continue to soften. ☙ When I make apricot jam, I add some apricot seeds to the saucepan to intensify the taste. The almond-shaped seed is in a hard shell, or "stone," which I crack. Apricot seeds, like bitter almonds, are high in prussic acid, which can be poisonous in large quantities, so they should never be consumed raw. Roasting them eliminates the problem and allows bitter almonds and apricot seeds to be used in almond flavorings and liqueurs. One liqueur, called *ratafia,* or another, made with fruit pits, called *noyau* in French, is sometimes added to almond paste to intensify its flavor.

Depending on their size, about eight to ten apricots make a pound. Each has only 15 to 18 calories and is high in vitamin A and fiber.

APRICOT AND FIG SOUFFLÉ

Flavored with a puree containing both dried apricots and apricot preserves, this soufflé has an intense taste that I like. Dried figs lend texture and provide interesting color contrast.

The soufflé will puff nicely and can be served hot in the mold. It also can be made ahead and served cold as a kind of apricot pudding. As it cools, it will deflate, falling to about the level of the uncooked mixture in the mold. It is good either way on its own, or it can be served with yogurt or sour cream.

6 *ounces dried apricots*
1 *cup water*
¼ *cup apricot preserves*
⅓ *cup diced dried figs (¼-inch dice)*
½ *teaspoon unsalted butter*
5 *egg whites*
1 *tablespoon granulated sugar*
 Confectioners' sugar (optional)
 Yogurt or sour cream (optional)

1. Place the apricots and water in a saucepan. Bring to a boil, cover, reduce the heat to low, and boil the mixture gently for 15 minutes. (All but about ⅓ cup of the water should have evaporated. If there is more, reduce it to this amount by boiling; if there is less, add enough water to make this amount.) Transfer the contents of the saucepan to the bowl of a food processor, add the preserves, and process until smooth.

2. Place the processed mixture in a bowl, fold in the figs, and set aside. (The recipe can be prepared to this point a few hours ahead.)

3. Preheat the oven to 375 degrees.

4. Grease a 4-cup soufflé mold with the butter, and set it aside.

5. About ½ hour before serving, beat the egg whites until stiff, add the granulated sugar, and beat for a few more seconds to incorporate it. Gently fold and mix the apricot mixture into the egg whites, and transfer the mixture to the buttered mold.

6. Bake for about 20 minutes, or until the soufflé is puffy and barely set inside. Sprinkle with the confectioners' sugar, if desired, and serve immediately, as is or with a spoonful of yogurt or sour cream on each serving, if you prefer.

YIELD
4 servings

TOTAL TIME
About 1 hour

NUTRITIONAL ANALYSIS PER SERVING
Calories 234
Protein 7 g
Carbohydrates 54 g
Fat 1 g
Saturated fat 0 g
Cholesterol 1 mg
Sodium 63 mg

APRICOT *FEUILLETÉ*

The dough base for this dessert is what I call "mock" puff pastry. Made with instant Wondra flour, it is prepared rapidly in a food processor, and the butter is incorporated in far fewer steps than are generally required to create the multiple layers characteristic of puff pastry. ✑ This is a recipe I prepare quite often, especially in winter, with canned apricots, which are appealingly sweet and often give me better results than fresh ones—unless I can find them ripe from the tree. Apricot halves are dried first in a hot oven to concentrate their flavor, then arranged on a rectangle of the puff pastry, and baked at a high temperature until the dough is well cooked and the apricots begin to brown. ✑ The number of apricots per can varies widely: some 16-ounce cans contain as few as eight, others as many as sixteen. Use large apricots, if possible, but follow the same procedures whatever the size of the fruit.

YIELD

8 servings

TOTAL TIME

About 2 hours

**NUTRITIONAL
ANALYSIS
PER SERVING**

Calories 226

Protein 2 g

Carbohydrates 37 g

Fat 8 g

Saturated fat 5 g

Cholesterol 23 mg

Sodium 50 mg

MOCK PUFF PASTRY

*1¼ cups instant Wondra flour
(about 4½ ounces)*

⅛ teaspoon salt

¼ teaspoon sugar

*¾ stick cold unsalted butter, cut into
6 slices (3 ounces)*

¼ cup ice water

2 cans (16 ounces each) apricot halves

FOR THE MOCK PUFF PASTRY

1. Place 1 cup of the flour in the bowl of a food processor with the salt, sugar, butter, and water. Process for 5 seconds. (The dough will not begin to gather together at this point, and pieces of butter will be visible throughout the mixture.)

2. Transfer the mixture to a cold surface (preferably marble). Using plastic wrap, gather it together, and press it into a rough mass. Sprinkle the dough and the rolling surface generously with some of the remaining ¼ cup of flour, and roll the dough into a rectangle about 14 by 5 inches.

3. Fold in the two narrow ends of the dough so they meet in the middle, then fold the dough again on this center meeting line to form a rectangle about 3½ by 5 inches.

4. Using more of the remaining flour, position the rectangle of dough so that one of the narrow ends faces you, and roll it again into a 14-by-5-inch rectangle. Repeat the folding procedure in step 3, wrap the resulting

5-by-3½-inch rectangle of dough in plastic wrap, and refrigerate it for at least 1 hour before proceeding.

FOR THE *FEUILLETÉ*

5. Meanwhile, preheat the oven to 350 degrees.

6. Drain the apricot halves, reserving the syrup in a small saucepan. Line a jelly roll pan with parchment paper, arrange the apricots cut side down on the paper, and bake them at 350 degrees for 30 to 40 minutes. Set them aside to cool until cooking time.

7. About 20 minutes before cooking time, preheat the oven to 400 degrees.

8. At cooking time, sprinkle the rolling surface with the remaining flour, roll the dough into a thin rectangle measuring 16 by 6 inches, and transfer it to a nonstick cookie sheet or a cookie sheet lined with a nonstick baking mat or parchment paper.

9. Arrange the apricot halves cut side down and side by side in rows on the pastry rectangle, keeping them about ¾ inch from the pastry edge on all sides. Fold the pastry edges back over the apricots to create a dough "container."

10. Bake the *feuilleté* at 400 degrees for about 40 minutes, or until the surface of the apricots is lightly browned and the dough is dark brown and crisp. Let the *feuilleté* cool for at least 15 minutes.

11. Meanwhile, bring the reserved syrup (about 1½ cups) to a boil over high heat, and boil until it is reduced to ⅓ cup.

12. Slide the cooled *feuilleté* onto a serving platter, and, using a pastry brush, glaze the apricots with the reduced syrup. Cool the dessert to room temperature, cut it into pieces, and serve.

Apricot Feuilleté *(these pages).*

MINTED APRICOT FONDUE WITH FRESH FRUITS

Colorful and multitextured, this fruit fondue makes an excellent party dessert. Each guest dips pieces of fresh and dried fruit in a sauce made of apricot preserves, minced mint leaves, and kirsch, a cherry brandy. You can also flavor the sauce with rum, cognac, or even whiskey, if you prefer, or eliminate the alcohol altogether.

YIELD
4 servings

TOTAL TIME
About 20 minutes

NUTRITIONAL
ANALYSIS
PER SERVING
Calories 428
Protein 3 g
Carbohydrates 107 g
Fat 1 g
Saturated fat 0 g
Cholesterol 0 mg
Sodium 38 mg

APRICOT DIPPING SAUCE

1 cup apricot preserves
2 tablespoons kirsch
1 tablespoon minced mint leaves
1 tablespoon water

1 ripe Anjou or Bartlett pear (about 7 ounces)
1 ripe peach (about 6 ounces)
½ pound strawberries (8 large), hulled and halved
2 teaspoons lemon juice
1 large seedless orange
12 dried Calimyrna figs (for information on Calimyrna figs, see introduction to Calimyrna Figs in Spicy Port Sauce, page 104)
⅓ cup dark muscat raisins
8 to 10 whole mint leaves, for garnish

1. In a small, attractive glass serving bowl, mix together the preserves, kirsch, minced mint leaves, and water. Set aside.

2. Peel the pear and the peach, if you like, and cut them lengthwise into quarters. Core the pear.

3. Place the pear, peach, strawberries, and lemon juice in a bowl, and toss gently to coat the fruit.

4. Halve the orange lengthwise, and cut each half crosswise into ⅜-inch slices.

5. At serving time, arrange the bowl of dipping sauce in the center of a platter, and surround it with the fresh and dried fruits. Garnish the fruit with the whole mint leaves, and serve the dessert, encouraging guests to dip the fruit pieces in the sauce.

Minted Apricot Fondue with Fresh Fruits (this page).

APRICOT COMPOTE

I love apricots in any form. For this recipe, I mix fresh apricots, processed with orange juice into a puree, with dried apricot strips, and then cook them together with a little honey and some pine nuts. The dessert is best served at room temperature with a garnish of sour cream or yogurt.

YIELD

4 servings

TOTAL TIME

About 20 minutes, plus cooling time

NUTRITIONAL ANALYSIS PER SERVING

Calories 252

Protein 7 g

Carbohydrates 50 g

Fat 5 g

Saturated fat 1 g

Cholesterol 1 mg

Sodium 28 mg

¾ *pound ripe fresh apricots (about 5)*
1 *cup orange juice*
5 *ounces dried apricot halves, cut into ½-inch strips (1¼ cups)*
¼ *cup pine nuts*
2 *tablespoons honey*
½ *cup sour cream or plain yogurt*

1. Pit the fresh apricots, and place the fruit in the bowl of a food processor with the orange juice. Process until the mixture is pureed, then transfer it to a saucepan.

2. Add the dried apricots, nuts, and honey to the saucepan, and bring the mixture to a boil over high heat. Reduce the heat to low, cover, and cook for 10 minutes, scraping the bottom of the pan with a spoon a few times to ensure that the mixture does not stick.

3. Cool the compote to room temperature, and divide it among four dessert bowls. Top each serving with a spoonful of sour cream or yogurt.

APRICOT *DÉLICE*

Délice is the French word for "delight," which accurately describes this fruit dessert. Fresh apricots are cooked in a sweet wine that is flavored with basil, and then cooled. With the addition of diced kiwi, the cooking liquid is transformed into a sauce and spooned over the apricots at serving time. (See photograph, page 103.)

½ cup apricot or peach preserves
1 cup Sauternes (sweet wine)
1 stalk fresh basil
2 tablespoons water
8 ripe apricots (1¼ pounds)
1 kiwi (about 3 ounces)
8 fresh basil leaves, for decoration

1. Place the apricot preserves, Sauternes, basil stalk, and water in a saucepan measuring about 7 inches across (just large enough to hold the apricots snugly in one layer). Bring the mixture to a boil, and add the apricots. (They should be barely covered with the liquid.) Bring the mixture back to a boil, cover, reduce the heat to low, and boil the apricots gently for 5 minutes, or until they are just tender. Let the apricots cool, covered, in the liquid.

2. Meanwhile, peel the kiwi, and cut the flesh into ¼-inch dice.

3. At serving time, arrange two apricots on each plate. Discard the basil stalk, and toss the kiwi pieces in the cooking juice. Coat the apricots with the juice, and divide the remaining juice and the kiwi pieces among the four plates. Decorate each apricot with a basil leaf, and serve.

YIELD
4 servings

TOTAL TIME
20 minutes

———

NUTRITIONAL ANALYSIS PER SERVING
Calories 211
Protein 2 g
Carbohydrates 44 g
Fat 1 g
Saturated fat 0 g
Cholesterol 0 mg
Sodium 21 mg

APRICOT AND HAZELNUT BISCOTTI

Biscotti, which keep for a long time, are great for snacks or desserts on their own or with fresh fruit. This recipe is easy: all the ingredients are mixed together for a few seconds in a food processor, shaped into a loaf, cooked in the oven for 30 minutes, then sliced and returned to the oven for 20 minutes more. The addition of dried apricots lends tangy taste and chewiness to the biscotti.

2   cups all-purpose flour
¾   cup sugar
¼   teaspoon salt
1   teaspoon baking powder
1   large egg
3   tablespoons milk
2   tablespoons canola oil
1½ teaspoons pure vanilla extract
¾   cup shelled hazelnuts or cashews
4   ounces dried apricots, cut into ¼-inch slices (⅔ cup)

1. Preheat the oven to 375 degrees.

2. Place the flour, sugar, salt, and baking powder in the bowl of a food processor, and process the mixture for 5 seconds. Add the egg, milk, oil, and vanilla, and process for 10 seconds, or until the mixture just begins to hold together.

3. Transfer the mixture to a bowl, add the nuts and apricots, and mix by hand until thoroughly combined.

4. Line a cookie sheet with parchment paper. Place the dough in a mound on a piece of plastic wrap about 18 inches long, and press to form it into a log about 12 inches long by 3 inches wide by 1 inch high. Invert the dough log onto the parchment paper, and peel off the plastic wrap. Bake the log at 375 degrees for 30 minutes, or until lightly browned on all sides and cracked on top. Cool on the cookie sheet for about 10 minutes. Meanwhile, reduce the oven heat to 350 degrees.

5. Transfer the log to a cutting board, and, using a serrated knife, cut it crosswise into ½-inch slices. (You should have about twenty-four.) Arrange the slices on the parchment-lined cookie sheet, and bake the biscotti at 350 degrees for 20 minutes, or until nicely browned on both sides. (There is no need to turn the biscotti over halfway through the baking time, as many biscotti recipes instruct; these brown nicely on both sides without turning.)

6. Cool the biscotti thoroughly on a wire rack, then store them in a dry place (or wrap them well, and freeze them).

Apricot and Hazelnut Biscotti (this page).

YIELD
4 servings

TOTAL TIME
About 1½ hours

———

NUTRITIONAL
ANALYSIS
PER COOKIE
Calories 60
Protein 1 g
Carbohydrates 9 g
Fat 3 g
Saturated fat 0 g
Cholesterol 5 mg
Sodium 42 mg

CHOCOLATE, WALNUT, AND APRICOT COOKIES

This oversized version of the traditional chocolate chip cookie also includes nuts and diced dried apricots. If you prefer, raisins can be substituted for the apricots—either dried fruit lends some acidity, which helps balance the sweetness of the chocolate. Most of this recipe can be assembled in the food processor in just a few minutes, with the chocolate chips, nuts, and dried fruit folded in just before the dough is dropped in large spoonfuls onto a cookie sheet and baked.

YIELD
About 20 cookies

TOTAL TIME
20 to 30 minutes

———

NUTRITIONAL ANALYSIS PER COOKIE
Calories 156
Protein 2 g
Carbohydrates 20 g
Fat 8 g
Saturated fat 2 g
Cholesterol 26 mg
Sodium 38 mg

⅔ *stick unsalted butter (5⅓ tablespoons)*
3 *tablespoons canola oil*
⅔ *cup light brown sugar*
2 *eggs*
2 *teaspoons pure vanilla extract*
1⅓ *cups all-purpose flour*
1 *teaspoon baking powder*
⅔ *cup walnut pieces*
⅓ *cup diced dried apricots (¼-inch dice)*
⅔ *cup semisweet chocolate morsels*

1. Preheat the oven to 375 degrees.

2. Place the butter, oil, sugar, eggs, and vanilla in the bowl of a food processor, and process the mixture for a few seconds, just until smooth. Add the flour and baking powder, and process just until they are incorporated and the dough is smooth, about 5 seconds.

3. Transfer the dough to a bowl, and, using a wooden spoon or spatula, stir in the nut and apricot pieces and the chocolate chips.

4. For each cookie, drop about 2 tablespoons of dough onto an ungreased cookie sheet, leaving about 2½ inches between the mounds. Bake for 8 to 10 minutes. Cool on a wire rack.

BAKED APRICOTS WITH ALMONDS

The success of this dish depends on the quality of the apricots you use. If you have very ripe, full-flavored fruit, preferably from an organic farm, you will have terrific results. I used to make this dessert with a lot of heavy cream; now I use just a little half-and-half. If you want to go one step further, eliminate the half-and-half, and add a few tablespoons of water to lend a little moisture to the fruit.

1   *pound ripe apricots (about 6 or 7)*
3   *tablespoons apricot jam*
¼   *cup half-and-half*
2   *tablespoons sliced almonds*
1   *tablespoon sugar*

1. Preheat the oven to 350 degrees.

2. Cut the apricots in half, and remove their pits.

3. Arrange the apricot halves cut side down in a gratin dish. Spoon the jam over the fruit, and pour the half-and-half around the fruit. Sprinkle the almonds and sugar on top.

4. Bake the apricots for 30 to 35 minutes. Serve the dessert lukewarm or at room temperature.

YIELD
6 servings

TOTAL TIME
About 45 minutes

———

NUTRITIONAL ANALYSIS PER SERVING
Calories 91
Protein 2 g
Carbohydrates 17 g
Fat 3 g
Saturated fat 1 g
Cholesterol 4 mg
Sodium 9 mg

BANANAS

In my culinary apprenticeship, in the early 1950s, the banana was relatively exotic and expensive. Now, it is second only to the apple in popularity and available year-round. Although there are many types of bananas, we are mostly familiar with the Cavendish, which has smooth yellow skin. The Burro banana is larger and has a thicker and darker skin, but its flesh is very lemony, creamy, and delicious. Other varieties, sometimes available in supermarkets, are the small-fingered red banana and the apple banana, which is about 5 inches long, thinner than the red variety, and very fragrant. ⌢ Bananas are a fruit that is picked green and ripens afterward. A bunch of bananas can weigh up to 50 pounds and consists of several "hands" hanging around a central stem. What you buy in the supermarket is a hand, consisting of about five fingers. Bananas are usually stored at room temperature, because they darken under refrigeration. Dried bananas, available in most markets, are very concentrated in taste. ⌢ In Hawaii, I saw chefs using the beautiful banana flowers. A large, oval, reddish cone, the bloom is made of tight leaves or petals that open to reveal tiny flowers at their bases. These sweet, edible flowers are used in island cooking. Asian markets offer an amazing variety of bananas; they are eaten and their large leaves are used

I like bananas when they have tiny brown specks on them, indicating ripeness and deeper flavor.

to wrap foods. ✑ Bananas are very high in potassium and vitamins A and C, and one standard-size banana has about 110 calories. Excellent eaten raw, bananas are delicious in savory dishes, too, particularly curries and other meat dishes. Mashed overripe bananas are very good in cakes, breads, and cookies. ✑ The plantain is a harder, larger type, used frequently in Caribbean cooking. Very ripe plantains are sliced and fried, then pounded, and fried again. They are conventionally used as a vegetable or a garnish for meat or fish.

LEMON BANANAS IN CRISP SHELLS

Instead of using rich cookie dough or puff pastry for the dessert shells here, I make them from packaged square wonton wrappers, which are fat-free. The wrappers are first blanched in boiling water, then lightly oiled, and baked until brown and crisp. When cool, the wrappers are filled, sandwich-style, with banana slices flavored with lemon juice and rind, dark rum, and peach preserves.

8   *wonton wrappers, each about 3 inches square (2 ounces total)*
2   *teaspoons canola oil*
1½ *tablespoons confectioners' sugar, plus 1 teaspoon for decoration*
2   *teaspoons grated lemon rind*
2   *tablespoons lemon juice*
¼   *cup peach preserves*
2   *tablespoons dark rum*
2   *ripe bananas (about 1 pound)*

1. Preheat the oven to 375 degrees.

2. Bring about 2 quarts of water to a boil in a pot. Drop in the wonton wrappers one at a time, and bring the water back to a boil. Boil the wrappers for 1½ minutes, then drain them carefully into a colander, and return them to the pot. Fill the pot with cold water to stop the wrappers from cooking further and cool them.

3. Brush a large cookie sheet with the oil. Using both hands, carefully lift the wrappers from the cold water, shaking off as much of the water clinging to them as you can, and arrange them side by side on the oiled sheet. Place the 1½ tablespoons of confectioners' sugar in a sieve, and sprinkle it on top of the wet wonton wrappers.

4. Bake the wrappers for 16 to 18 minutes, until they are nicely browned, crisp, and glazed on the surface. Using a thin hamburger spatula, transfer them to a rack to cool completely.

5. Meanwhile, mix the lemon rind, lemon juice, peach preserves, and rum in a bowl large enough to hold the bananas. Peel the bananas, and cut them in half crosswise, then into thin (⅓-inch) lengthwise slices. Add them to the bowl, and mix gently to coat the slices with the sauce.

6. At serving time, arrange a wonton crisp on each of four dessert plates. Divide the banana mixture among the plates, spooning it on top of the crisps. Place the remaining wonton crisps on top of the bananas, and sprinkle the remaining teaspoon of sugar on top. Serve immediately.

YIELD
4 servings

TOTAL TIME
45 to 60 minutes

———

NUTRITIONAL ANALYSIS PER SERVING
Calories 209
Protein 2 g
Carbohydrates 42 g
Fat 3 g
Saturated fat 0 g
Cholesterol 1 mg
Sodium 92 mg

BANANA–RASPBERRY SHERBET
WITH RASPBERRY SAUCE

This easy dessert is a sherbet made without an ice-cream maker. Bananas give creaminess and body to the dish and complement the intensity of the berries. Do not freeze this mixture until it is very hard, or, if you're making it a day ahead, let it defrost a little to soften slightly before trying to emulsify it in a food processor. If possible, process the sherbet just before serving; last-minute processing makes it especially creamy and smooth.

YIELD

4 servings

TOTAL TIME

About 20 minutes, plus freezing time

———

NUTRITIONAL ANALYSIS PER SERVING

Calories 185

Protein 1 g

Carbohydrates 45 g

Fat 1 g

Saturated fat 0 g

Cholesterol 0 mg

Sodium 11 mg

1   package (12 ounces) individually quick-frozen (IQF) raspberries, defrosted
⅓   cup seedless raspberry preserves
1   tablespoon raspberry brandy
3   ripe bananas (about 1 pound)
4   sprigs of mint or 4 edible flowers, for decoration

1. Push the defrosted berries and raspberry preserves through a food mill fitted with the finest screen. Remove any remaining seeds by straining the mixture through a sieve with a medium (not too fine) mesh. (You should have about 1¾ cups of sauce.) Divide the sauce into two portions, 1 cup and ¾ cup. Stir the brandy into the ¾ cup of sauce, and set it aside.

2. Peel and slice the bananas, and mix them with the remaining 1 cup of sauce. Transfer the mixture to a gratin dish, and place it in the freezer. At the same time, refrigerate the bowl of a food processor to chill it. Freeze the banana mixture, stirring occasionally, until it is firm but not frozen hard.

3. Transfer the frozen banana mixture to the chilled food processor bowl, and process for about 30 seconds. Return the sherbet to the cold gratin dish, and serve it immediately, or place it back in the freezer until serving time.

4. To serve, divide the sherbet among four bowls. Garnish each serving with a generous spoonful of the raspberry sauce, and decorate each with a sprig of mint or an edible flower.

BANANA–MINT ICE CREAM WITH RAISIN–RUM SAUCE

This is a great dessert to prepare when you have several overripe bananas languishing in your fruit bowl. The recipe is easy: slice the bananas, freeze them on a tray, then puree them in a food processor along with some honey, mint, and sour cream. Store this almost instant ice cream in the freezer for several hours before serving it with a delicious sauce made of peach preserves, orange juice, rum, and raisins.

BANANA–MINT ICE CREAM

3 ripe bananas (about 1½ pounds), peeled
¼ cup honey
6 to 8 mint leaves
¾ cup sour cream

RAISIN–RUM SAUCE

¼ cup peach preserves
¼ cup orange juice
1 tablespoon dark rum
¼ cup golden raisins

4 strips fresh mint (optional)

FOR THE BANANA–MINT ICE CREAM

1. Cut the bananas into ½-inch slices, and arrange them in a single layer on a cookie sheet. Place in the freezer for at least 2 hours.

2. Remove the bananas from the freezer, and allow them to soften slightly at room temperature for a few minutes. Place the bananas (still frozen but not solid) in the bowl of a food processor, and add the honey, mint, and sour cream. Process for at least 1 minute, until the mixture is smooth and creamy. (You should have about 3½ cups.)

3. Transfer the mixture to a bowl, cover, and freeze for several hours, until solidly frozen.

FOR THE RAISIN–RUM SAUCE

4. In a small bowl, mix the preserves, orange juice, and rum together until smooth. Stir in the raisins.

5. At serving time, spoon the ice cream into four bowls, and coat with the sauce. Decorate each serving with a mint strip, if you like.

Banana–Mint Ice Cream with Raisin–Rum Sauce (this page).

YIELD
4 servings

TOTAL TIME
10 minutes, plus about 5 hours' freezing time

NUTRITIONAL
ANALYSIS
PER SERVING
Calories 332
Protein 3 g
Carbohydrates 62 g
Fat 9 g
Saturated fat 5 g
Cholesterol 19 mg
Sodium 28 mg

BANANA FRITTERS

The nearer to serving time you cook the fritters, the better; they emerge from the oil crunchy and crusty, thanks to the addition of ice water, which makes the fritter batter resemble a tempura batter. If you must cook the fritters ahead, remove them from the hot oil, drain them on a rack, and either serve them at room temperature or place them under the broiler for a few minutes to make them warm and crisp again. Dust the fritters with sugar just before serving.

YIELD
4 servings

TOTAL TIME
About 30 minutes

———

NUTRITIONAL ANALYSIS PER SERVING
Calories 329
Protein 3 g
Carbohydrates 40 g
Fat 19 g
Saturated fat 2 g
Cholesterol 0 mg
Sodium 2 mg

¾ cup all-purpose flour
¾ teaspoon baking powder
1¼ cups ice water
    About 1 cup canola oil, for frying
2 ripe bananas
    About ⅓ cup granulated or
    confectioners' sugar

1. Place the flour, egg, and about half the water in a bowl. Mix with a whisk for a few seconds, until the mixture is smooth, and then whisk in the remainder of the water.

2. To cook the fritters, in a large, nonstick skillet, heat ⅓ cup of the oil to about 400 degrees. Meanwhile, peel the bananas, and, holding them directly over the bowl containing the batter, cut them crosswise into ¼-inch slices (let the slices fall into the batter).

3. Make three or four fritters at a time, using about ⅓ cup of the batter for each and pouring it into the hot oil. Spread the mixture lightly as it hits the pan to create fritters about 3 inches in diameter. Cook for 3 to 4 minutes, turn, and cook for 3 to 4 minutes on the other side, until nicely browned.

4. Remove the fritters with a slotted spoon, and place them on a wire rack to drain. Continue to make fritters, adding more oil as needed, until all the batter has been used.

5. Sprinkle the drained fritters generously with sugar, and serve them as soon as possible.

Banana Fritters (this page).

BANANA TARTLETS

You can make these tartlet shells up to a day ahead but don't fill them with the pastry cream and fruit until just before serving. You can eliminate the pastry cream altogether, if you prefer, and fill the shells with the sliced bananas or another fresh fruit.   This tartlet dough recipe contains only ½ cup of flour, 3 tablespoons of butter, and 1½ teaspoons of oil, which is remarkably little, considering it serves four. Since a quarter to a third of the dough will be trimmed away when it is pressed into shells for baking, an even smaller amount of these ingredients will actually be consumed in this dessert. The pastry cream is similarly deceptive: although it contains 1 cup of milk, it has only 1 egg yolk and 1 tablespoon of cornstarch, so it is much less caloric than a conventional pastry cream.

YIELD

4 servings

TOTAL TIME

About 50 minutes, plus cooling time

NUTRITIONAL ANALYSIS PER SERVING

Calories 427

Protein 5 g

Carbohydrates 71 g

Fat 14 g

Saturated fat 7 g

Cholesterol 85 mg

Sodium 40 mg

TARTLET SHELLS

½   cup all-purpose flour

3   tablespoons unsalted butter

1½ teaspoons canola oil

1½ teaspoons sugar

1   tablespoon milk

PASTRY CREAM

1   cup milk

1   egg yolk

2   tablespoons sugar

1   teaspoon pure vanilla extract

1   tablespoon cornstarch

TOPPINGS

1   large ripe banana (10 ounces)

½   cup apricot preserves

1   tablespoon kirsch

4   dried dates, pitted and thinly sliced

FOR THE TARTLET SHELLS

1. Preheat the oven to 400 degrees.

2. Place the flour, butter, oil, and 1½ teaspoons of sugar in the bowl of a food processor, and process the mixture for 10 seconds. Add the 1 tablespoon of milk, and process just until the mixture forms a ball.

3. Transfer the dough to a board, and roll it between two sheets of plastic wrap to form an 8-inch square approximately ⅛ inch thick. Arrange four tartlet shells (3 inches in diameter by ½ inch deep) side by side in two rows on your countertop. Remove the sheet of plastic wrap from the top of the dough, and, supporting the dough with the plastic wrap underneath, invert it over the tartlet shells.

4. Peel off the remaining sheet of plastic wrap, and use it to press the dough lightly into the shells. Then run your rolling pin directly over the tops of the shells to trim away excess dough. Remove and reserve the dough trimmings. (They will amount to about a quarter of the dough.)

5. To make the dough adhere well to the bottoms and sides of the shells, dust your hands lightly with flour, and press the dough firmly into each shell. To prevent the dough from collapsing while cooking, line each of the shells with wax paper or aluminum foil, and fill them with rice or lead pellets. Or, if you have enough extra shells, press an empty one lightly into each of the pastry-lined shells to hold the dough in position during cooking. Arrange the shells on a cookie sheet. Either wrap the reserved dough trimmings well and refrigerate or freeze them for later use, or lay them flat on a cookie sheet and bake them with the tartlets to eat as a snack.

6. Bake the tartlets for 10 minutes. Remove the empty shells or weight-filled wax paper or foil, and bake the pastry for 5 minutes longer, or until it is nicely browned. Unmold the tartlets onto a wire rack, and cool.

FOR THE PASTRY CREAM

7. Bring the 1 cup of milk to a boil in a saucepan.

8. Meanwhile, whisk the egg yolk, 2 tablespoons of sugar, vanilla, and cornstarch together in a bowl. Then whisk this mixture into the boiling milk, and cook, stirring constantly, for 1 minute. Transfer the pastry cream to a bowl, cool to room temperature, cover, and refrigerate until just before serving time.

FOR THE TOPPINGS

9. At serving time, fill the pastry shells with the pastry cream. Slice the banana, and arrange the slices over the pastry cream in the tartlets. In a small bowl, combine the apricot preserves and kirsch, and spoon the mixture over the bananas. Sprinkle the dates on top, and serve.

BROILED BANANAS WITH LEMON AND SUGAR

The best bananas for this dish are those with skin speckled with black dots, indicating that the fruit is very ripe. Since bananas are often moved to the quick-sale rack when they reach this stage, look for them there at greatly reduced prices. If your bananas are slightly underripe or you like your desserts very sweet, you may want to add 1 or 2 more tablespoons of brown sugar to compensate for their tartness.

YIELD

4 servings

TOTAL TIME

10 minutes,
plus cooling time

**NUTRITIONAL
ANALYSIS
PER SERVING**

Calories 177

Protein 1 g

Carbohydrates 43 g

Fat 1 g

Saturated fat 0 g

Cholesterol 0 mg

Sodium 7 mg

4   *ripe bananas, about 6 ounces each*
    (1½ pounds total)
¼   *cup fresh lemon juice*
¼   *cup dark brown sugar*
1   *tablespoon golden raisins*
1 to 2 *tablespoons dark rum*

1. Preheat the broiler.

2. Peel the bananas, and arrange them in one layer in a gratin dish. Pour the lemon juice over the bananas, and roll them in the juice to prevent them from discoloring. Sprinkle the brown sugar evenly over them.

3. Broil the bananas about 4 inches from the heat, until they are brown on top, about 4 minutes. Turn the bananas, and broil them again for 3 to 4 minutes, until they are brown on top. At this point, they should be soft when pierced with a fork. Scatter the raisins over them.

4. Cool the bananas until they are lukewarm, sprinkle them with the rum, and shake the dish to mix in the rum. Serve immediately.

Broiled Bananas with Lemon and Sugar (this page).

BAKED BANANAS IN LEMON–RUM SAUCE

Available year-round, bananas are best when little black spots begin to form on the skins, indicating that they are very ripe. For this recipe, the bananas are baked in their skins, which blacken completely after 15 minutes of cooking. When they are cool enough to handle, the fruit is removed from the skin and served with the tart lemon–rum sauce (or simply with a little lemon juice).

4 *very ripe bananas, with black-spotted skin (about 2 pounds)*

LEMON–RUM SAUCE

1 *tablespoon grated lemon rind*
2 *tablespoons lemon juice*
2 *tablespoons sugar*
3 *tablespoons orange marmalade*
¼ *cup water*
2 *tablespoons dark rum*

GARNISHES

Mint leaves
Strips of orange peel

1. Preheat the oven to 400 degrees.

2. Trim about ½ inch from each end of the bananas, and cut a slit through the skin extending the length of the fruit. Arrange the unpeeled bananas on a cookie sheet, and bake them for 15 minutes. (The skins will turn black.)

3. Meanwhile, in a saucepan, mix together the lemon rind, lemon juice, sugar, marmalade, and water, and bring the mixture to a boil. Boil for 1 minute. Transfer this sauce to a serving dish large enough to hold the bananas.

4. As soon as the bananas are cool enough to handle, remove the skins, and place the bananas in the sauce. Using a spoon, coat the bananas on all sides with the sauce.

5. When the bananas are cool, stir in the rum, and decorate the bananas with the mint leaves and orange peel. Serve one whole banana per person with some of the sauce and garnishes.

YIELD
4 servings

TOTAL TIME
About 45 minutes

———

NUTRITIONAL
ANALYSIS
PER SERVING
Calories 216
Protein 2 g
Carbohydrates 52 g
Fat 1 g
Saturated fat 0 g
Cholesterol 0 mg
Sodium 10 mg

BLACKBERRIES, BLUEBERRIES, AND CRANBERRIES

There are many kinds of blackberries; the more elongated ones are sometimes called black mulberries, and others are known as elderberries, boysenberries, and loganberries. My friends and I didn't recognize any of these distinctions, however; they were all *mûres* to us. ᔆ Like most berries, blackberries are high in fiber and relatively low in calories—about 70 in a full cup. They are perishable, and washing them tends to fill them with water, which makes them spoil faster. Remember that they render a great deal of liquid when cooked. Blackberries are usually available from May to September.

Blueberries, one of the most common fruits at the market, are high in vitamin C. The United States and Canada are enormous producers of blueberries. Wild blueberries, which are smaller than cultivated varieties, are available from about May to October; they have a more intense taste and a firmer texture than the cultivated ones. Occasionally, when walking in the woods in search of mushrooms, I find low-bush blueberries, which grow wild. These tiny berries are much blacker than supermarket varieties and very good. ᔆ A versatile fruit, blueberries are delicious raw and great cooked in pies and jams. When purchasing blueberries, select firm specimens that have a silvery, frostlike skin color. Avoid washing

Blackberries remind me of my childhood experiences picking "mûres" in France.

51

fresh berries until just before you are ready to use them (although water doesn't penetrate them as readily as it does blackberries). Blueberries can sometimes be found dried or frozen at the supermarket. They freeze well, but will bleed and be very soft when defrosted; they can't be eaten out of hand in this condition but are fine for pies.

Most markets sell fresh cranberries in 12-ounce plastic bags, and they are quite inexpensive.

Cranberries are best in the fall. The biggest harvests come from Massachusetts and Wisconsin, which supply close to 200 million pounds a year. The berries also grow wild in parts of northern Europe and North America, including Canada. The peak growing months are from September to January. ➿ It is said that the Pilgrims ate cranberries at the first Thanksgiving dinner. While jellied cranberry sauce is a standard today for Thanksgiving, I would rather make a chutney with fresh or frozen cranberries. Yet my wife insists on having canned cranberry jelly with her turkey. ➿ High in vitamin C and fiber, cranberries have only about 50 calories to a cup, but they need a lot of sugar, because they are tart—too tart to eat raw. They cook in just a few minutes, releasing their juice and mixing readily with seasonings. ➿ Choose cranberries that are plump and bright. Stored in the refrigerator, they will keep for at least a month, in the bag or, as some people recommend, covered with water.

TRIPLE LAYERS OF BLACKBERRIES AND KIWIS WITH HONEY–ARMAGNAC SAUCE

This is an easy, colorful, and delicious dessert. The blackberries and kiwis can be replaced with whatever fruits are available, from bananas to peaches, strawberries, or raspberries. You can make your own pound cake or buy a good-quality pound cake at your market.

2   tablespoons lemon juice
2   tablespoons Armagnac or, if unavailable, cognac or bourbon
¼   cup honey
2   kiwis (9 ounces total), peeled and cut into ¼-inch-thick crosswise slices (16 to 20 slices)
2   cups blackberries (about 8 ounces)
12 slices pound cake about ¼ inch thick and 2½ inches square

1. Mix the lemon juice, Armagnac, and honey in a bowl until well combined. Add the kiwi slices and blackberries, and stir gently to coat the fruit with the honey mixture. Cover, and set the fruit aside to marinate until serving time (up to a few hours later or as soon as you complete the dish).

2. Arrange a slice of pound cake on each of four dessert plates. Sprinkle a few blackberries on top of and around the cake, and add one or two slices of kiwi. Sprinkle with some of the juice from the bowl.

3. Repeat step 2 twice more on each plate to make three layers of cake, fruit, and juice. Pour any remaining juice on top of and around the desserts, and serve immediately.

YIELD
4 servings

TOTAL TIME
About 15 minutes, plus marinating time

NUTRITIONAL ANALYSIS PER SERVING
Calories 332
Protein 4 g
Carbohydrates 54 g
Fat 11 g
Saturated fat 6 g
Cholesterol 74 mg
Sodium 126 mg

BLACKBERRIES IN CREAMY HONEY SAUCE

For this dessert, ripe blackberries are tossed in a little sugar and mounded on plates coated with a sauce composed of honey, orange juice, yogurt, and mint. Quick and easy, the dish is as attractive as it is flavorful. Any other berries—strawberries, raspberries, boysenberries—can be substituted here. Be sure to choose very ripe berries for maximum sweetness.

YIELD

4 servings

TOTAL TIME

10 minutes,
plus chilling time

**NUTRITIONAL
ANALYSIS
PER SERVING**

Calories 137

Protein 4 g

Carbohydrates 31 g

Fat 0 g

Saturated fat 0 g

Cholesterol 1 mg

Sodium 44 mg

2   *cups blackberries (1 pint)*
1   *tablespoon sugar*
3   *tablespoons honey*
¼   *cup orange juice*
1   *cup nonfat plain yogurt*
1   *tablespoon shredded fresh
      peppermint leaves*

1. Gently toss the blackberries and sugar in a small bowl. Cover, and refrigerate until serving time.

2. Meanwhile, mix the honey and orange juice in another small bowl. When the mixture is smooth, add the yogurt and mint, and mix just until smooth. Cover, and refrigerate until serving time.

3. To serve, divide the yogurt sauce among four dessert plates. Mound some berries in the center, dividing them equally among the plates. Serve immediately.

BLUEBERRIES WITH BROWN SUGAR

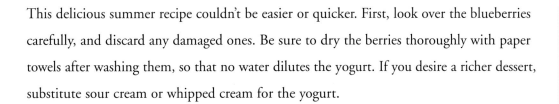

This delicious summer recipe couldn't be easier or quicker. First, look over the blueberries carefully, and discard any damaged ones. Be sure to dry the berries thoroughly with paper towels after washing them, so that no water dilutes the yogurt. If you desire a richer dessert, substitute sour cream or whipped cream for the yogurt.

1   *pint blueberries, washed and dried*
8   *tablespoons plain yogurt*
4   *tablespoons dark brown sugar*
    Mint leaves, for garnish

1. Divide the blueberries among four plates. Make a well in the center of the berries on each plate, and spoon in about 2 tablespoons of the yogurt.

2. Sprinkle the berries and yogurt with the brown sugar, decorate with a few mint leaves, and serve. The sugar will melt and spread somewhat on the yogurt, giving the dessert an interesting look.

YIELD

4 servings

TOTAL TIME

5 minutes

———

NUTRITIONAL
ANALYSIS
PER SERVING

Calories 110

Protein 1 g

Carbohydrates 25 g

Fat 1 g

Saturated fat 1 g

Cholesterol 4 mg

Sodium 23 mg

CUSTARD WITH BLUEBERRY SAUCE

Prepared with milk and a minimum of sugar, this custard is quite lean. On its own, it might not be as rich-tasting as you would like, but in combination with a sauce of fresh blueberries, good-quality apricot preserves, and cognac, it makes a beautiful dessert.

The water bath surrounding the custard molds as they bake should not be allowed to boil, or the custard will overcook. If the water begins to boil, add a few ice cubes (removing enough water to compensate for the ice as it melts) to quickly lower the water temperature. Remove the molds from the oven as soon as the custard is lightly set yet still somewhat jellylike if shaken. It will continue to firm as it cools.

CUSTARD

2   large eggs
¼   cup sugar
1   teaspoon pure vanilla extract
1¾ cups milk

BLUEBERRY SAUCE

¼   cup apricot preserves,
     best possible quality
2   tablespoons cognac
1   tablespoon water (optional)
1   cup fresh blueberries

FOR THE CUSTARD

1. Preheat the oven to 350 degrees.

2. Break the eggs into a mixing bowl, and beat them with a fork until they are well combined and there is no visible sign of egg white. Add the sugar, vanilla, and milk, and mix well to dissolve the sugar.

Top: Potted Plums with Phyllo Dough (see page 160); bottom: Custard with Blueberry Sauce (this page).

3. Arrange four small (¾-cup) soufflé molds in a roasting pan, and strain the custard mixture into the molds. Surround the molds with enough lukewarm tap water to extend about three-quarters of the way up the sides of the molds.

4. Place the pan in the oven, and bake the molds for about 35 minutes, until the custard is barely set. Remove the molds from the water bath, and refrigerate them for at least 3 hours.

FOR THE BLUEBERRY SAUCE

5. Mix the preserves and cognac together in a small bowl, adding the water, if needed, to thin the mixture to the consistency of a sauce. Stir in the blueberries, and set aside.

6. At serving time, unmold the custards on individual plates, spoon some blueberry sauce over and around them, and serve immediately.

YIELD

4 servings

TOTAL TIME

45 minutes,
plus chilling time

———

NUTRITIONAL
ANALYSIS
PER SERVING

Calories 240
Protein 7 g
Carbohydrates 37 g
Fat 6 g
Saturated fat 3 g
Cholesterol 120 mg
Sodium 94 mg

BLUEBERRY CRUMBLE

I especially like this easy recipe made with blueberries, but blackberries, boysenberries, and raspberries are also good like this, flavored with a fruit preserve or jam, moistened with a little orange juice, and topped before baking with leftover cake or cookie crumbs. The crumble can be served on its own, with yogurt, or (if you want to splurge) with sour cream or whipped cream.

YIELD

4 servings

TOTAL TIME

About 40 minutes

———

NUTRITIONAL ANALYSIS PER SERVING

Calories 234

Protein 5 g

Carbohydrates 39 g

Fat 7 g

Saturated fat 2 g

Cholesterol 35 mg

Sodium 70 mg

2 cups fresh or frozen blueberries (about 10 ounces)

¼ cup apricot preserves

2 tablespoons orange juice

3 ounces pound cake, sponge cake, or cookies, crumbled

1 cup yogurt

1. Preheat the oven to 375 degrees.

2. Mix the blueberries, preserves, and orange juice together in a bowl, then transfer the mixture to a 3-cup gratin dish.

3. Crumble the cake or cookies on top, covering the blueberries entirely, and bake for 30 minutes.

4. Serve the crumble lukewarm, topped with about 2 generous tablespoons of yogurt per person.

BLUEBERRIES *AU CITRON*

For this recipe, blueberries are flavored simply with lemon juice and maple syrup. I make this dessert only when fresh blueberries are readily available, and whenever possible I use the tiny wild berries, which I find more flavorful than the large cultivated ones.

1   *lemon*
¼   *cup maple syrup*
1   *pint blueberries (12 ounces),*
    preferably small wild ones

1. Using a vegetable peeler, remove four strips of peel from the lemon, and set them aside. Cut the lemon in half, and squeeze it to obtain the juice (about 2 tablespoons).

2. Mix the lemon juice and maple syrup in a bowl large enough to hold the blueberries.

3. Rinse the blueberries in cool water, removing and discarding any stems, debris, and damaged berries. Drain the berries well, and add them to the syrup mixture along with the lemon peel. Mix thoroughly, and refrigerate for at least 1 hour before serving.

YIELD
4 servings

TOTAL TIME
5 minutes,
plus chilling time

——

NUTRITIONAL
ANALYSIS
PER SERVING
Calories 95
Protein 1 g
Carbohydrates 24 g
Fat 0 g
Saturated fat 0 g
Cholesterol 0 mg
Sodium 6 mg

Blueberries au Citron *(this page).*

RUSSIAN CRANBERRY *KISSEL*

Kissel is a classic Russian dessert that usually consists of a puree of acidic fruit. Any tart berries can be used, but cranberries are the traditional choice. Sometimes the berries are merely combined with sugar and thickened with a little cornstarch. I add orange juice and rind to my version and serve the *kissel* with a little yogurt (or, if I want it richer, sour cream) and garnishes of pomegranate seeds and mint. For an easy way to remove seeds from a pomegranate, see step 2 of Papaya Segments with Tangerine *Sabayon* and Pomegranate Seeds on page 217.

YIELD

4 servings

TOTAL TIME

About 30 minutes,
plus cooling time

———

NUTRITIONAL
ANALYSIS
PER SERVING

Calories 181

Protein 2 g

Carbohydrates 45 g

Fat 1 g

Saturated fat 0 g

Cholesterol 2 mg

Sodium 13 mg

1   package (12 ounces) fresh cranberries
1½ teaspoons grated orange rind
¾   cup orange juice
½   cup sugar
1   teaspoon cornstarch
¼   cup plain yogurt or sour cream
2   tablespoons pomegranate seeds
    A few sprigs mint
4   cookies (optional)

1. Pick over the cranberries, and discard any damaged ones. Place the cranberries, orange rind, orange juice, sugar, and cornstarch in a stainless steel saucepan, and bring the mixture to a boil over high heat, stirring occasionally. Cover, reduce the heat to low, and cook gently for about 10 minutes. The mixture will be thick and bright red. Set it aside to cool. (You should have about 2 cups.)

2. When the *kissel* cools, divide it among four glass goblets. Garnish with the yogurt or sour cream, a sprinkling of the pomegranate seeds, and the mint. Serve with the cookies, if desired.

Left: Frozen Black Velvet (see page 105); center: Grapefruit and Kiwi Ambrosia (see page 81); right: Russian Cranberry Kissel *(this page).*

CRANBERRY SOUFFLÉS WITH CRANBERRY–RED WINE SAUCE

Fresh cranberries, available at supermarkets much of the year now, are used in this dessert. The berries are cooked first with a little sugar and jam. Some of the mixture is then pureed and combined with wine to create a flavorful sauce, and the remainder is folded into egg whites for the soufflé. Small, disposable aluminum molds can be used, or the soufflés can be baked in conventional glass, ceramic, or metal molds. ⌣ The assembled soufflés can be cooked immediately, of course, but they also can be refrigerated for a few hours, or even frozen, before cooking. If you decide to make them ahead and freeze them, transfer the frozen molds directly from the freezer to the hot oven, and cook the soufflés as indicated in the recipe. (See photograph, page 112.)

(See photograph, page 112.)

YIELD

4 servings

TOTAL TIME

About 1 hour, plus optional chilling or freezing time

NUTRITIONAL ANALYSIS PER SERVING

Calories 265

Protein 3 g

Carbohydrates 52 g

Fat 3 g

Saturated fat 2 g

Cholesterol 8 mg

Sodium 6 mg

---

1   *tablespoon unsalted butter (to butter the molds)*
1   *10-ounce package fresh cranberries*
⅓   *cup granulated sugar*
½   *cup apricot or peach jam*
¼   *cup water*
¾   *cup fruity, dry red wine*
3   *egg whites*
    Confectioners' sugar

1. If you will bake the soufflés immediately after preparing them, preheat the oven to 375 degrees.

2. Butter four ¾-cup aluminum, ovenproof glass, or ceramic molds. Set them aside.

3. Combine the cranberries, granulated sugar, jam, and water in a large stainless steel saucepan, and bring the mixture to a boil over medium-to-high heat. Cover the saucepan, reduce the heat to very low, and cook the mixture gently for 20 minutes. (You will have about 1¾ cups.)

4. Place ¾ cup of the cranberry mixture in the bowl of a food processor, and process it until smooth. Add the red wine, process briefly, and strain the mixture through a fine strainer set over a bowl. Set the sauce aside until serving time.

5. Beat the egg whites until they are firm. Working as quickly as you can, fold them into the remaining cup of cooked cranberries. Fill the prepared molds with the mixture, and smooth the tops with a spatula. If desired, mound the excess mixture in the center of each soufflé to create a decorative "knob" (see photograph, page 112). Either bake the soufflés immediately, refrigerate them for up to 2 hours before baking, or freeze them (uncovered until firm, then covered) for up to 2 weeks before baking.

6. If you are baking the soufflés immediately or after a brief refrigeration, arrange the filled molds on an aluminum tray, and bake them at 375 degrees for 13 to 15 minutes, or until they are puffy on top and set in the center. If you are baking frozen soufflés, place them on a tray directly from the freezer, and bake in a preheated 375-degree oven for 15 to 18 minutes. (If the soufflés begin to darken on top after 10 to 12 minutes, place a sheet of aluminum foil loosely on top of them for the remainder of the cooking period.) When they are done, sprinkle the hot soufflés with the confectioners' sugar.

7. To serve the soufflés, divide the sauce among four plates. Using a large scoop, scoop the soufflés from the molds, and place one in the center of each plate. Serve immediately.

CHERRIES

The cherry, which was domesticated in China more than four thousand years ago, is a favorite fruit. Its tree is so beautiful in bloom that people flock to Washington, DC, each spring to see the flowering ornamental ones. ∽ There are two basic types, the sweet and the sour, with hundreds of varieties. Sweet cherries are generally available from early June on; the sour ones arrive around the middle of July. Most sweet cherries in the market are Bing cherries, which are very large, round, deep red to almost black in color, and delicious for eating fresh. As a child in France, I picked and ate sweet Royal Ann and Rainier cherries, both pinkish-blue with a little yellow. ∽ The Montmorency, probably the best known of the sour varieties, is small, very juicy, and light red. Although it is good fresh from the tree, it is usually cooked in jams or pies and is sometimes pickled in vinegar. When I can get Montmorency cherries with stems, I often preserve them in alcohol to serve as an after-dinner "drink." If the stems are removed, however, the alcohol gets inside the fruit and makes it mushy. ∽ Choose cherries that are shiny, round, and plump, with light green stems (darker stems indicate age). Keep cherries at room temperature or refrigerate them in a plastic bag, and don't wash them until just before using. ∽ Cherries have a fair

I have a neat little machine for pitting cherries (and olives), but you can also pit them by hand, using the point of a knife or even a paper clip.

amount of fiber and contain vitamin C. Be advised that the leaves of cherry trees are poisonous and should not be used, even as a garnish. ⁐ Frozen and dried cherries are also available in markets. *Cerises glacées* are candied cherries, and Maraschino cherries are cherries that are dyed, flavored, and kept in a syrup. They do not resemble fresh cherries even remotely in taste, and I tend to avoid them. Some brandy is made from cherries; the most famous is kirsch, in which some of the pits are cracked and added to the macerating cherries to give the brandy a specific taste. The best kirsch comes from northeastern France, Lorraine and Alsace, and from the Black Forest. A type of cherry liqueur, misleadingly called cherry brandy, is also used in cooking and in desserts. ⁐ Nothing matches the big, crunchy, reddish-yellow cherries I enjoyed as a kid. My brother and I called them *bigarreaux,* and we ate them ripe from the tree in our backyard in France. My mother still has the tree, and it still yields a great many cherries, year after year.

CHERRY BREAD PUDDING

This is a great dessert to prepare when Bing cherries are in full season. You can make the same recipe with berries or pieces of plum instead of cherries, and flavor them with the almond–sugar mixture, too. The pudding is best served lukewarm, with a little sour cream or yogurt, if you wish.

½ *cup sliced almonds*
1 *pound ripe cherries, rinsed and drained*
3 *slices white bread (3 ounces), toasted*
1 *cup milk*
½ *cup cherry preserves*
4 *teaspoons granulated sugar*
1 *teaspoon unsalted butter*
½ *teaspoon confectioners' sugar*
1 *cup sour cream or yogurt (optional)*

1. Preheat the oven to 350 degrees. Spread the almonds on a cookie sheet, and bake them for 8 to 10 minutes, or until lightly browned. Leave the oven on.

2. Pit the cherries. Coarsely crumble the toasted bread (you should have 1 cup), place it in a bowl with the milk, and mix well. Add the cherries, all but 2 tablespoons of the almonds, and the cherry preserves.

3. In another bowl, mix the reserved 2 tablespoons of almonds with 2 teaspoons of the granulated sugar.

4. Grease a 6-cup gratin dish with the butter, and sprinkle it with the remaining 2 teaspoons of granulated sugar. Pour the cherry mixture into the dish, and top it with the almond–sugar mixture.

5. Bake the pudding for 35 to 40 minutes. Cool it to lukewarm, sprinkle it with the confectioners' sugar, and serve it with the sour cream or yogurt, if desired.

YIELD
6 servings

TOTAL TIME
About 1 hour,
plus cooling time

———

NUTRITIONAL
ANALYSIS
PER SERVING
Calories 322
Protein 6 g
Carbohydrates 44 g
Fat 15 g
Saturated fat 7 g
Cholesterol 24 mg
Sodium 128 mg

TOP-CRUST CHERRY PIE

This is an easy way of making a large cherry pie. Sweetened cherries are baked in a gratin dish with a layer of dough on the top only. To serve the pie, you cut pieces of the crisp brown crust, invert them onto dessert plates, and pile the baked cherries on top. ᕱ If fresh cherries are not available, substitute unsweetened, individually quick-frozen (IQF) cherries.

FILLING

2 pounds large Bing cherries, or a mixture of Bing, Rainier (Golden Bing), and Montmorency cherries, pitted (about 5½ cups, or 1 pound, 10 ounces, pitted weight)
⅔ cup sugar
2 tablespoons potato starch
1 teaspoon pure vanilla extract
½ teaspoon pure almond extract

DOUGH

¾ cup all-purpose flour
2 tablespoons unsalted butter
1½ tablespoons sugar
    Pinch of salt
6 tablespoons cottage cheese

    Ice cream, sour cream, or plain yogurt (optional)

1. Preheat the oven to 375 degrees.

2. Place the filling ingredients in a bowl. Mix well, and transfer the mixture to a 5-cup round or oval gratin dish.

3. Place the dough ingredients in the bowl of a food processor. Process for 15 to 20 seconds, or until the mixture begins to come together.

4. Transfer the dough to a piece of plastic wrap 3 to 4 inches larger than the gratin dish, and form the dough into a ball in the center of the wrap. Place another piece of plastic wrap on top of the dough, then roll the dough out to form a circle or an oval (depending on the shape of your gratin dish) about 1 inch larger all around than the dish.

5. Peel the top piece of plastic wrap from the surface of the dough, and, holding the edges of the remaining piece of wrap, invert the dough over the gratin dish so it hangs down about 1 inch beyond the sides of the dish. Peel off the remaining piece of plastic wrap.

(CONTINUED)

Top-Crust Cherry Pie (this page).

6. Carefully lift the dough overhang with your fingers, and roll it onto itself to create a thicker layer of dough all around the edge of the dish. Then, using your thumb and fingers, press on the thick dough edge to seal it to the dish and create a decorative border.

7. Prick the dough in the center a few times with a sharp knife to allow steam to escape, and place the gratin dish on a cookie sheet. Bake the pie for 45 minutes, covering it with aluminum foil for the last 10 minutes, if necessary, to prevent the crust from becoming too brown. Cool the pie to room temperature on a rack.

8. To serve, break through the crust with a spoon, and arrange a section of crust on each of six plates. Spoon a portion of the filling on top of or alongside the crust. Serve with a small scoop of ice cream or a tablespoon of sour cream or plain yogurt, if desired.

CHERRY COMPOTE

I like to make this dessert in summer, when large Bing cherries are available and excellent in quality. I first pit the cherries and then, to concentrate their flavor, cook them along with the cracked pits in a sturdy white wine flavored with cherry jam. The pits give the fruit a slightly bitter, almondlike taste that I find particularly appealing.

1¼ *pounds large Bing cherries,*
stems removed
¾ *cup sturdy white wine (such as*
chardonnay)
3 *tablespoons sugar*
¼ *cup cherry jam*
1 *teaspoon cornstarch dissolved in*
1 tablespoon water
1 *tablespoon kirsch (optional)*
4 *tablespoons sour cream*
Cookies (optional)

1. Pit the cherries, and reserve the pits. Place the pitted cherries, wine, sugar, and jam in a stainless steel saucepan.

2. Arrange the reserved cherry pits on a piece of plastic wrap set on a cutting board, and cover them with another piece of plastic wrap. Using a meat pounder or the base of a small, heavy saucepan, pound the pits to crack them. Transfer the cracked pits to a piece of cheesecloth, and tie them into a compact package. Add the package to the cherry mixture in the saucepan.

3. Bring the cherry mixture to a boil, cover, reduce the heat to low, and boil the mixture gently for 5 minutes. Add the dissolved cornstarch, and mix well. Cool. Remove and discard the package of pits, and stir in the kirsch, if desired.

4. Serve the compote in glass goblets with 1 tablespoon of sour cream on top of each serving and, if desired, a few cookies.

YIELD
4 servings

TOTAL TIME
About 15 minutes,
plus cooling time

———

NUTRITIONAL
ANALYSIS
PER SERVING
Calories 240
Protein 2 g
Carbohydrates 43 g
Fat 1 g
Saturated fat 1 g
Cholesterol 6 mg
Sodium 19 mg

SUMMER CHERRY PUDDING
WITH RUM SAUCE

This cherry pudding is a classic summer offering in England. Sour cherries are cooked briefly in wine and sugar, then layered with cake crumbs in a bowl lined with pound cake. After a few hours, the juices from the cherry mixture seep into the cake, and the dessert becomes a solid mass that takes on the shape of the bowl. Unmolded at serving time, it is presented here with a sauce made of mango, honey, and rum.

CHERRY PUDDING

1½ pounds sour cherries
½   cup dry, fruity red wine
¼   cup sugar
1   10¾-ounce pound cake

RUM SAUCE

1   ripe mango (about 1 pound)
2   tablespoons honey
1   tablespoon dark rum
⅓   cup water

⅓   cup champagne grapes, if available, or Red Flame grapes cut into ¼-inch pieces, for garnish

FOR THE CHERRY PUDDING

1. Pit the cherries, and place them in a stainless steel saucepan with the wine and sugar. Bring the mixture to a boil, uncovered, over medium heat, and cook for 5 minutes to reduce the juices. Cool. (You will have 2¼ cups.)

2. Trim off the brown exterior of the pound cake, and reserve the trimmings. Cut the trimmed cake lengthwise into five slices, each about ½ inch thick.

3. Place a long strip of parchment paper about 2 inches wide in a 4- to 6-cup bowl so that the paper covers most of the bottom, comes up the sides, and extends a little beyond the edge of the bowl. (This will help in the unmolding later.) Arrange three slices of the cake on top of the parchment so that the cake covers the bottom and sides of the bowl.

(CONTINUED)

YIELD

4 servings

TOTAL TIME

45 to 50 minutes, plus chilling time

_____

NUTRITIONAL
ANALYSIS
PER SERVING

Calories 432

Protein 5 g

Carbohydrates 74 g

Fat 13 g

Saturated fat 7 g

Cholesterol 135 mg

Sodium 249 mg

Summer Cherry Pudding with Rum Sauce (this page).

4. Place half the cherry mixture on top of the cake, and crumble half the reserved cake trimmings over the cherries. Spoon the remaining cherry mixture on top, and crumble the remaining cake trimmings over it. Finish with the remaining two slices of cake, arranging them so that all the cherries are covered.

5. Cover the bowl with plastic wrap touching the cake. Place a weight of about 1 pound on top of the dessert to press and compact the layers of cake and cherries. Refrigerate. (The recipe can be prepared to this point up to 2 days ahead.)

FOR THE RUM SAUCE

6. Peel the mango, and cut the flesh from the pit. Place the flesh in a food processor or blender with the honey, rum, and water, and process until smooth. (You will have 1¾ cups.)

7. When you are ready to serve the pudding, unmold it onto a serving plate and discard the parchment. Pour the mango sauce around the pudding, and decorate the plate with the grapes. Spoon the pudding and sauce onto dessert dishes at the table.

GÂTEAU AUX CERISES (CHERRY CAKE)

I like to prepare this dessert when cherries are plentiful and inexpensive at the market. Often, we buy fruit and don't eat it within a few days, so it starts getting soft and a bit wilted. This recipe is an excellent vehicle for slightly "tired" cherries and a reminder that we can usually find ways to use overripe fruits.

1½ *pounds sweet or sour cherries (Bing, Royal Ann, or Montmorency)*

3 *tablespoons unsalted butter, softened*

1 *tablespoon canola oil*

½ *cup granulated sugar*

¼ *teaspoon almond flavoring (optional)*

2 *large eggs*

1 *cup all-purpose flour (about 5½ ounces)*

1½ *teaspoons baking powder*

½ *cup milk*

Confectioners' sugar, for sprinkling on the cake just before serving

1. Pit the cherries, and set them aside.

2. Preheat the oven to 375 degrees.

3. Place the butter, oil, and granulated sugar in a bowl, and mix them together well with a whisk. Add the almond flavoring, if desired, and the eggs, and mix them in thoroughly. Add the flour and baking powder, and mix with the whisk until smooth. Add the milk, and stir just enough to make a smooth batter.

4. Butter a 9-by-2-inch round cake pan. Add the cherries to the batter, mix them in gently but thoroughly, and pour the batter into the pan.

5. Place the pan on a cookie sheet in the oven. Bake for 45 minutes, or until the cake is nicely browned on top and bounces back when tapped lightly in the center.

6. Cool to lukewarm, sprinkle with confectioners' sugar, cut into wedges, and serve.

YIELD

6 to 8 servings

TOTAL TIME

About 1¼ hours

NUTRITIONAL ANALYSIS PER SERVING (8 SERVINGS)

Calories 255

Protein 5 g

Carbohydrates 40 g

Fat 9 g

Saturated fat 4 g

Cholesterol 67 mg

Sodium 117 mg

SWEET CHERRY AND BERRY TARTLETS WITH RASPBERRY SAUCE

This dessert is composed of three recipes: one is for the tartlet shells, one is for the fruit filling (although the tartlets could be filled with chocolate or lemon curd instead), and one is for the raspberry sauce, which could also be frozen into a sherbet. The fruit filling mixture—a good dessert on its own—can be changed to use the fresh fruits available at your market. ✍ Heating a lime in a microwave oven, as I do here, breaks down the fiber holding the juice and yields a greater amount of juice than the conventional approach—pressing on the lime with your hand—before cutting and squeezing it. This microwave technique can be applied to any citrus fruit.

YIELD

6 servings

TOTAL TIME

About 1 hour

NUTRITIONAL ANALYSIS PER SERVING

Calories 537

Protein 10 g

Carbohydrates 104 g

Fat 9 g

Saturated fat 5 g

Cholesterol 53 mg

Sodium 73 mg

TARTLET SHELLS

¾ cup all-purpose flour (about 4 ounces)

½ stick unsalted butter (2 ounces)

1 tablespoon light brown sugar

1 tablespoon granulated white sugar

⅛ teaspoon salt

1 egg yolk

1 tablespoon water

FRUIT FILLING

1 small lime

1 cup blueberries

1½ cups cleaned and halved strawberries

8 ounces cherries, pitted (about 1¼ cups)

¼ cup sugar

RASPBERRY SAUCE

1½ cups fresh or frozen raspberries

6 ounces (half a 12-ounce jar) seedless blackberry jam

1½ tablespoons kirsch

GARNISHES

Sour cream (optional)

6 sprigs mint

FOR THE TARTLET SHELLS

1. Place the flour, butter, sugars, and salt in the bowl of a food processor, and process for 10 seconds. Add the egg yolk and water, and process for another 5 seconds or until the mixture starts to come together. Press the dough into a ball.

2. Group six small round, rectangular, or oval molds with sides about ½ inch high (mine are 4-by-2-inch rectangular molds) together on your kitchen countertop. Roll the dough between pieces of plastic wrap to a thickness of approximately 1¼ inches. Peel off the top sheet of plastic wrap, and invert the rolled dough over the tops of the assembled tartlet molds. Using your fingers or a crushed ball of plastic wrap, press the dough firmly into the molds so it adheres well, and trim excess dough from the sides of the molds. Prick the dough with a fork, and line each mold with aluminum foil, pressing it lightly but firmly against the dough to hold the dough in place and prevent it from collapsing during baking. Arrange the molds on a cookie sheet, and refrigerate them until the dough is cold. (The recipe can be prepared to this point a day ahead.)

3. Shortly before you are ready to bake the shells, preheat the oven to 375 degrees. When it is hot, bake the shells, still lined with aluminum foil, for 15 minutes. Remove the cookie sheet from the oven momentarily (closing the door to maintain the oven temperature), and discard the aluminum foil pieces. (By now, the dough is set and will not collapse or shrink.)

4. Return the cookie sheet to the oven, and bake the tartlets for another 12 to 15 minutes, or until they are nicely browned and cooked throughout. Cool them on a rack, then remove them from the molds.

FOR THE FRUIT FILLING

5. Heat the lime in a microwave for 45 seconds. Allow it to cool.

6. Squeeze the lime juice into a bowl. (You should have 2 tablespoons.) Add the blueberries, strawberries, cherries, and sugar, and combine. Cover and refrigerate. (You should have about 5 cups.)

FOR THE RASPBERRY SAUCE

7. Place the raspberries and jam in the bowl of a food processor. Process for a few seconds, or until the mixture is pureed. Strain through a sieve, and stir in the kirsch. (You should have about 1¾ cups.)

8. At serving time, divide the sauce among six cold dessert plates. Place a tartlet shell in the center of each plate, on top of the sauce, and fill it with the fruit mixture, letting the berries spill over the shell. Top each dessert with a tablespoon of sour cream, if desired, and decorate with a sprig of mint.

GRAPEFRUITS, LEMONS, AND ORANGES

The grapefruit is a relatively new fruit, available commercially only since the 1900s. Florida is the largest producer of grapefruits. My favorite variety is the juicy, pink-fleshed seedless type that a friend sends me every winter from Florida. When you are purchasing grapefruit, select heavy fruit with smooth yellow skin. Grapefruit makes wonderful sherbet, and large segments of the fruit are excellent with a berry sauce.

Select lemons that are deep yellow and limes that are deep green. Choose thin-skinned specimens, especially to use for juice. You can extract almost twice as much juice if you first drop lemons or limes in boiling water or microwave them for 30 seconds, to break down their texture inside. Another method is to roll the uncut fruit on a hard surface, pressing it with the palm of your hand to crack the fibers. Lemon and lime juices are often used to flavor desserts and to retain the color of other fruits, such as apples and pears.

There is nothing like freshly squeezed orange juice at the beginning of the day. It is an excellent source of vitamin C; in fact, an 8-ounce glass meets the entire daily requirement. Above all, it is absolutely delicious. Since fruits are often sprayed with wax and sometimes colored on the outside, color does not necessarily indicate ripeness. Some types of oranges that are

The juice of lemons and limes is used as a tenderizer for meats and fish since it can coagulate the protein.

still slightly green around the stem are extremely juicy, ripe, and flavorful. ∽ Most of the oranges we eat in this country come from Florida. When I use oranges for juice, I use the least expensive Valencia type, but the best variety to eat raw or use as segments in desserts is the seedless navel (or "bellybutton") orange.

Select oranges (and other citrus fruits) that are heavy, because the weight usually indicates the amount of juice.

The citrus family includes kumquats, mandarins, tangerines, tangelos (a mixture of grapefruit and tangerine), and ugli fruit. All citrus fruits will keep under refrigeration for a couple of weeks. ∽ Of all the fruits, lemons, limes, oranges, and grapefruits may be the most versatile. They are used not only in desserts but also in main dishes, such as stews, or to enhance the flavor of veal, for example, and in numerous alcoholic drinks. ∽ The calorie count for a large orange is about 70; a lemon is much less, about 15, and a lime contains about 20. Oranges, tangerines, and the like are what doctors call "detergent fruits" because eating their pulp helps clean the teeth.

GRAPEFRUIT AND KIWI AMBROSIA

This refreshing, satisfying dessert is the ideal finish for an elegant menu. The grapefruit is cut into membrane-free wedges and mixed with pieces of kiwi and sweet white Sauternes-type wine. Intensely flavored Sauternes, the greatest dessert wine in the world, is made from grapes attacked by the fungus *botrytis,* which shrivels them and concentrates the flavor of their juice. This wine can also be served with the dessert. (See photograph, page 61.)

2   *Ruby Red grapefruits (1 pound each)*
3   *kiwis*
½   *cup Sauternes-type sweet white wine*
2   *tablespoons Grand Marnier liqueur*
8   *Bing cherries*

1. Peel the grapefruits with a sharp knife, removing all the skin and underlying white pith so that the flesh of the fruit is totally exposed. Cut between the membranes, and remove the flesh in wedgelike pieces. Place the grapefruit pieces in a bowl, and squeeze any remaining juice from the membranes over them before discarding the membranes.

2. Peel the kiwis, and cut them into ½-inch pieces. Add them to the grapefruit along with the wine and Grand Marnier. Mix, and allow the fruit to macerate for at least a few minutes and as long as a few hours before serving.

3. To serve, spoon the fruit into four glass goblets or dessert dishes, and top each serving with a couple of the cherries.

YIELD
4 servings

TOTAL TIME
About 20 minutes

———

NUTRITIONAL ANALYSIS PER SERVING
Calories 119
Protein 1 g
Carbohydrates 22 g
Fat 1 g
Saturated fat 0 g
Cholesterol 0 mg
Sodium 4 mg

CRÊPE SOUFFLÉS IN GRAPEFRUIT SAUCE

These crêpes can be made ahead and served unstuffed on their own, with the grapefruit sauce, or with jam. In this recipe, I fill them with a low-calorie soufflé mixture made from a combination of stiffened, slightly sweetened egg whites and grated grapefruit rind. This same mixture could be baked without the crêpes in a large greased soufflé mold (1½- or 2-quart size) for approximately 30 minutes and then served with the grapefruit sauce alongside. ⌒ I use a very light crêpe batter that contains only one egg and cook the crêpes in an 8-inch nonstick skillet. Perhaps the most important thing to remember when making crêpes is to spread the batter very quickly in the hot skillet so it will not solidify before it coats the bottom of the pan; if you move too slowly, you will need more batter, and the resulting crêpe will be too thick. Use a twisting, tilting, and shaking motion to move the batter quickly over the surface of the pan, coating it lightly.

GRAPEFRUIT SAUCE

1   Ruby Red grapefruit (1 pound)
¼   cup grenadine syrup
1   tablespoon lemon juice

CRÊPES

½   cup all-purpose flour
1   egg
¾   cup milk
2   tablespoons canola oil plus
    ¼ teaspoon for greasing skillet
⅛   teaspoon salt
¼   teaspoon sugar

SOUFFLÉ MIXTURE

5   egg whites
¼   cup sugar
1   tablespoon grated grapefruit rind
    (from grapefruit used in sauce)
1   teaspoon unsalted butter
6   fresh mint leaves, coarsely chopped,
    for garnish (optional)

1. Grate the grapefruit skin (colored part only, not white pith) to obtain 1 tablespoon of rind. Reserve.

(CONTINUED)

YIELD
6 servings

TOTAL TIME
About 1 hour

NUTRITIONAL ANALYSIS PER SERVING
Calories 198
Protein 6 g
Carbohydrates 27 g
Fat 7 g
Saturated fat 2 g
Cholesterol 41 mg
Sodium 118 mg

Crêpe Soufflés in Grapefruit Sauce (this page).

FOR THE GRAPEFRUIT SAUCE

2. Peel the remaining skin and white pith from the grapefruit. With a sharp knife, remove the flesh segments from all surrounding membranes. Squeeze the membranes to obtain ½ cup of juice.

3. Cut the segments into ½-inch pieces (about ½ cup), and combine them in a bowl with the grapefruit juice, grenadine, and lemon juice.

FOR THE CRÊPES

4. In a bowl, mix the flour, the egg, and ¼ cup of the milk with a whisk until very smooth. Add the remaining milk, the 2 tablespoons of oil, the salt, and the ¼ teaspoon of sugar, and mix well.

5. With the remaining oil, lightly grease the bottom of an 8-inch nonstick skillet, and place it over high heat. When it is hot, add 3 tablespoons of batter, and tilt and shake the skillet quickly until the batter covers the entire bottom of the pan.

6. Cook the crêpe for 45 seconds, turn it over, and cook it for 30 seconds on the other side. Continue making crêpes, stacking them on a plate as they are done, until all the batter is gone.

FOR THE SOUFFLÉ MIXTURE

7. Preheat the oven to 375 degrees.

8. Beat the egg whites until firm. Add the ¼ cup of sugar and the reserved grapefruit rind all at once, and beat for another 15 to 30 seconds.

9. Lightly butter six 1½-cup ovenproof glass bowls. Line each bowl with a crêpe, and spoon soufflé mixture into the center. Fold the edges of the crêpe up over the soufflé mixture to enclose it.

10. Arrange the bowls on a baking tray, and bake them for 8 minutes.

11. To serve, unmold the soufflés, and arrange them browned side down (or up, if you prefer) on individual plates. Spoon some sauce around each soufflé, and, if desired, garnish with the chopped mint leaves.

GRAPEFRUIT GRATIN

~

This easy, flavorful dessert can be prepared ahead up to the cooking step. The broiling is best done at the last moment, so that the grapefruit sections are warm, soft, and slightly caramelized on top when served.

2   grapefruits, preferably pink (about 1 pound each)
3   tablespoons light brown sugar
1   tablespoon unsalted butter
1   tablespoon cognac (optional)

1. Using a sharp, thin-bladed knife, remove the skin and underlying pith from each grapefruit, leaving the fruit totally exposed. Cut between the membranes on each side of the grapefruit segments, and remove the flesh in wedgelike pieces. You should have about twenty-four wedges. Squeeze the membranes over a bowl to extract the juice, and drink this at your leisure.

2. Arrange the grapefruit sections in one layer in a gratin dish. When you are ready to complete the dish, preheat the broiler.

3. Sprinkle the grapefruit segments with the sugar, and dot them with the butter. Place the dish about 4 inches under the heat in the broiler, and broil for 5 minutes to brown the edges of the segments lightly. If desired, sprinkle with the cognac, and serve immediately.

YIELD
4 servings

TOTAL TIME
15 minutes

———

NUTRITIONAL ANALYSIS PER SERVING
Calories 99
Protein 1 g
Carbohydrates 19 g
Fat 3 g
Saturated fat 2 g
Cholesterol 8 mg
Sodium 4 mg

Grapefruit Gratin (this page).

GRAPEFRUIT IN NECTAR

Wedgelike pieces of grapefruit flesh are removed from their surrounding membranes and served in a sauce composed of the juice squeezed from the membranes, a caramel, and—for added flavor—grenadine and Cointreau. For best results, use large, flavorful pink grapefruits for this recipe.

YIELD

4 servings

TOTAL TIME

About 30 minutes, plus cooling time

—

NUTRITIONAL ANALYSIS PER SERVING

Calories 100

Protein 1 g

Carbohydrates 24 g

Fat 0 g

Saturated fat 0 g

Cholesterol 0 mg

Sodium 0 mg

2 *pink grapefruits (2 pounds)*
1½ *cups water*
¼ *cup sugar*
2 *tablespoons water*
1 *tablespoon grenadine syrup*
1 *tablespoon Cointreau or other liqueur to your liking*

1. Using a vegetable peeler, remove six strips of grapefruit peel from areas of the fruit where the skin color is brightest. Stack the strips together, and cut them lengthwise into long, thin julienne strips. (You should have about ¼ cup.) Place the julienne in a small, high-sided saucepan, add the 1½ cups of water, and bring to a boil. Boil for 20 seconds, then drain the strips, and rinse them in a sieve held under cold, running water. Drain them well, and set them aside in a small bowl.

2. Using a sharp knife, peel the grapefruit, removing and discarding all the remaining skin and cottony pith, so that the flesh of the fruit is totally exposed. Then cut between the membranes on each side of the grapefruit segments, and remove the flesh in wedgelike pieces. You should have ten to twelve completely clean segments (without

any thin surrounding membrane) per grapefruit. Place these in a bowl, and sprinkle the blanched julienne on top. Squeeze the membranes through a sieve set over a bowl, pressing them to release as much juice as possible. Reserve this juice. (You should have ⅓ to ½ cup.)

3. Place the sugar and the 2 tablespoons of water in a small saucepan, bring the mixture to a boil, and boil it over high heat for about 3 minutes, or until it becomes a dark blond caramel. Remove the pan from the heat, and carefully add 1 or 2 tablespoons of the reserved grapefruit juice (the hot caramel will splatter). Shake the pan to mix. Add the rest of the juice, and mix well with a whisk until the juice is incorporated.

4. Pour the caramel sauce over the grapefruit segments in the bowl, and mix well. Add the grenadine and Cointreau, and mix again. Cover, and refrigerate until serving time. The recipe can be prepared to this point up to 8 hours ahead.

5. To serve, lift the grapefruit segments from the bowl with a slotted spoon, and divide them among four dessert plates. Pour the sauce over and around them, and serve.

CANDIED GRAPEFRUIT, ORANGE, AND LEMON CHIPS

This is a great Christmas holiday recipe, yielding delicacies that are quite inexpensive to make but expensive to buy. Slices of Ruby Red grapefruit, seedless orange (or thinner-skinned Florida orange, if you prefer), and lemon (and/or lime) are arranged on baking trays, sprinkled with sugar, and dried in a low-temperature oven until they are slightly hardened but still somewhat chewy. The slices will keep almost indefinitely if stored in an airtight container.

1   *Ruby Red grapefruit (about 1 pound)*
1   *large seedless orange (about 12 ounces)*
1   *large lemon (about 9 ounces)*
5   *tablespoons sugar*

1. Preheat one or two ovens to 200 degrees. (See step 4, below.)

2. Cut the grapefruit crosswise into ten slices, each ¼ inch thick, and discard the end pieces. Line a jelly roll pan with aluminum foil, and arrange the grapefruit slices in one layer in the pan. Sprinkle the slices with 2 tablespoons of the sugar.

3. Repeat step 2 with the orange and lemon, cutting each into about ten slices and sprinkling them all with the remaining 3 tablespoons of sugar.

4. Bake the pans on two separate racks in the preheated oven (or use two ovens, if available) for 3½ to 4 hours, until the slices are dried and candied but not browned. Remove them immediately from the pans, and cool them to room temperature on a rack.

5. Store the citrus chips in a plastic container, tightly covered. Serve them as a garnish or snack.

YIELD
About 30 chips

TOTAL TIME
About 5 hours

—

NUTRITIONAL ANALYSIS PER CHIP
Calories 17
Protein 0 g
Carbohydrates 5 g
Fat 0 g
Saturated fat 0 g
Cholesterol 0 mg
Sodium 0 mg

LEMON MOUSSE WITH CANDIED LEMON SLICES

My wife enjoys condensed milk, which reminds her of dishes her mother made when she was a child. I add some of this milk to the lemon mousse to give it a creamier and richer consistency. The candied lemon slices intensify the lemon character of the dish.

LEMON MOUSSE

⅓ cup sugar

5 tablespoons cold water

3 egg yolks

1½ tablespoons grated lemon rind

1 envelope plain gelatin (about 2 teaspoons)

1 cup heavy cream

⅓ cup fresh lemon juice

7 ounces (half a 14-ounce can) sweetened condensed milk

CANDIED LEMON SLICES

1 lemon (about 5 ounces)

7 cups water

⅓ cup sugar

1 tablespoon rum (optional)

Berries, edible flowers, or mint leaves for garnish (optional)

FOR THE LEMON MOUSSE

1. Combine the sugar with 3 tablespoons of the cold water in a saucepan. Bring the mixture to a boil, and boil it for about 2 minutes, or until it is a light syrup.

2. Meanwhile, place the yolks in the bowl of an electric mixer. Add the lemon rind, and beat on low speed while you slowly add the hot sugar syrup. Increase the speed to high, and continue beating for 10 minutes.

3. While the mixer is beating the yolk mixture, place the remaining 2 tablespoons of cold water in a small ovenproof glass dish, and sprinkle the gelatin on top. Place the dish in a small skillet, add water to the skillet extending about halfway up the sides of the dish, and heat the water, while stirring the mixture occasionally, until the gelatin has melted.

4. Whip the cream in a mixing bowl until soft peaks form. Set aside.

5. When the yolk mixture is ready, add the lemon juice and melted gelatin to it, and mix well. Using a whisk, mix in the condensed milk. Finally, fold in the whipped cream quickly but thoroughly. (You should have 4 cups of the mixture.) Transfer the mousse to a glass or ceramic serving bowl large enough so that the mousse is no more than 3 inches thick in the dish; alternatively, divide the mousse among individual dessert bowls or tulip glasses. Cover and refrigerate the mousse while you make the candied lemon slices.

(CONTINUED)

Left: Lemon Mousse with Candied Lemon Slices (this page); right: Oranges in Orange "Baskets" (see page 90).

YIELD

6 to 8 servings

TOTAL TIME

About 1 hour

—

NUTRITIONAL ANALYSIS PER SERVING (8 SERVINGS)

Calories 275

Protein 4 g

Carbohydrates 33 g

Fat 15 g

Saturated fat 9 g

Cholesterol 129 mg

Sodium 47 mg

FOR THE CANDIED LEMON SLICES

6. Cut the lemon crosswise into very thin (⅛-inch) slices, using a mandoline or a very sharp knife. (You should have eighteen to twenty slices.) Discard any seeds.

7. Bring 3 cups of the water to a boil in a medium saucepan. Immediately add the lemon slices, and bring the water back to a boil. Boil for 5 seconds, then drain the lemon in a sieve, and rinse it under cold water for a few seconds.

8. Wash the saucepan, and repeat step 7 a second time.

9. Wash the saucepan again, and return the lemon slices to the pan with the sugar and the remaining 1 cup of water. Bring the mixture to a boil, then reduce the heat to low, and boil it very gently for 30 minutes. (At this point, there should be about ¼ cup of syrup remaining around the lemon slices.) Cool, and stir in the rum, if desired.

10. At serving time, arrange the lemon slices on top of the mousse. Pour on the syrup, and decorate each serving, if desired, with a berry, an edible flower, or mint leaves.

ORANGES IN ORANGE "BASKETS"

Since this is the simplest of fresh fruit desserts—half an orange, plain except for a berry or mint sprig garnish—it is imperative that you use good-quality seedless oranges. The unusual presentation makes it easy to extract and enjoy the orange pieces. (See photograph, page 88.)

2   seedless oranges (6 to 8 ounces each)
4   strawberries, raspberries, or mint sprigs

1. Cut a ½-inch slice from both the stem end and the flower end of each orange, and set these slices aside.

2. Cut each orange in half crosswise. Using a paring knife, cut all around the flesh in each half, and remove the flesh in one thick piece from the surrounding cottony pith. You will have four disks of orange flesh and four hollow orange halves, or receptacles, to use as baskets.

3. Gently press a reserved end slice flesh side up into each orange basket to create a lining. Quarter each disk of orange flesh, and place

YIELD
4 servings

TOTAL TIME
10 to 15 minutes

NUTRITIONAL
ANALYSIS
PER SERVING
Calories 53
Protein 1 g
Carbohydrates 13 g
Fat 1 g
Saturated fat 0 g
Cholesterol 0 mg
Sodium 1 mg

the quarters back in the orange baskets in their original form, arranging them to simulate the appearance of an uncut orange half.

4. Decorate each orange basket with a berry or a sprig of mint, and serve one basket per person, with toothpicks for removing the orange pieces easily.

ORANGES IN GRAND MARNIER

In this refreshing dessert, oranges are poached just briefly and flavored with Grand Marnier. Make the dish far enough ahead so that the oranges can cool completely in the cooking syrup. Julienned orange rind, blanched first to eliminate bitterness, lends texture and intensifies the orange taste.

4   seedless navel oranges (6 ounces each)
3   cups water
¼   cup sugar
2   tablespoons Grand Marnier liqueur
    Mint leaves, for garnish

1. With a vegetable peeler, cut ten long strips of peel, each about 1 inch wide, from the oranges. Stack the strips, and cut them lengthwise into a julienne (very thin strips). Set aside 1 tablespoon of the strips for a garnish. Place the remaining julienne in a large saucepan, cover with 2 cups of the water, and bring to a boil. As soon as the mixture boils, drain the julienne in a colander, rinse it under cool water, rinse the saucepan, and return the julienne to the pan with the remaining cup of water and the sugar. Cook for 3 to 4 minutes, stirring occasionally, until large bubbles form and the mixture becomes a syrup.

2. Finish peeling the oranges, removing the white pith under the skin as well. Cut the oranges in half crosswise, and add them to the syrup. Cover, and cook over low heat for 3 to 4 minutes, checking occasionally and adding 1 or 2 tablespoons of water if no liquid is visible in the pan.

3. Let the oranges cool in the syrup, then add the Grand Marnier. Arrange two orange halves and some syrup in each dessert dish. Garnish with the reserved orange julienne and some mint leaves.

YIELD
4 servings

TOTAL TIME
30 minutes,
plus cooling time

**NUTRITIONAL
ANALYSIS
PER SERVING**
Calories 124
Protein 1 g
Carbohydrates 29 g
Fat 0 g
Saturated fat 0 g
Cholesterol 0 mg
Sodium 1 mg

CANDIED ORANGE RIND

This is an inexpensive treat made simply from orange skins and sugar. I peel skin from whole oranges here, but you can save skins from oranges as you use them over a period of days and set them aside in the refrigerator until you are ready to candy them. The candied rind will keep for several weeks in an airtight container, remaining dry on the outside and moist inside.   ⤳   Be sure to blanch the rind, rinse it well, and clean the pan before cooking the rind in the sugar; otherwise it will be too bitter.   ⤳   If any syrup remains after the rind is cooked, use it as a flavoring for pastry cream or cake.

YIELD

4 servings
(about 3 dozen pieces)

TOTAL TIME

About 1 hour

———

**NUTRITIONAL
ANALYSIS
PER SERVING**

Calories 32

Protein 0 g

Carbohydrates 8 g

Fat 0 g

Saturated fat 0 g

Cholesterol 0 mg

Sodium 0 mg

2   large seedless navel oranges (1¼ pounds)
1¼ cups sugar
4   cups cold water

1. Using a vegetable peeler, peel the oranges from the stem end to the navel end, removing eight to ten strips of peel about 1 inch wide from each orange.

2. Cut each strip in half lengthwise. You should have about three dozen strips ½ inch wide.

3. Place the strips in a saucepan, add about 6 cups of water, and bring to a boil. Boil for 5 seconds, drain, and rinse the strips under cool water. Wash the pan, and return the strips to it with ¾ cup of the sugar and the 4 cups of cold water. Bring to a boil over high heat, and boil over medium-to-high heat for about 40 minutes, or until the rind is transparent and the syrup has thickened but not darkened. Remove the pan from the heat.

4. Spread the remaining ½ cup of sugar on a cookie sheet. With a fork, transfer the orange peels from the pan to the cookie sheet. Press them into the sugar to coat them with it on all sides. Arrange the peels in a single layer on a plate, and allow them to dry for 1 hour. Store them in an airtight container.

ORANGE AND GRAPEFRUIT SEGMENTS

This is an attractive dish, especially if you use blood oranges, which contrast nicely with the grapefruit. In addition to using the flesh of the fruits, I mix the juice squeezed from the fruit membranes with a little honey to create a sauce. Garnished with mint and julienned orange skin, this makes a delightful dinner dessert with a slice of sponge cake or with cookies.

2   *seedless navel or blood oranges*
    (8 to 10 ounces each)
2   *Ruby Red grapefruits (1 pound each)*
2   *tablespoons honey*
    Mint leaves, for garnish
2   *tablespoons julienned orange skin,*
    for garnish

1. With a vegetable peeler, remove about six strips of peel from one of the oranges, and cut the strips into a fine julienne. Remove and discard the rest of the peel (including the white pith underneath) from the oranges and the grapefruits.

2. With a sharp knife, remove the orange and grapefruit segments from between their membranes, and then squeeze the membranes into a bowl to release the juices. (You should have 1 cup of combined juices.) Whisk the honey into the juice until combined.

3. Arrange alternating segments of orange and grapefruit in four dishes, and pour the sweetened juice over them. Garnish with mint leaves and julienned orange peel. Serve cold.

YIELD
4 servings

TOTAL TIME
About 20 minutes

**NUTRITIONAL
ANALYSIS
PER SERVING**
Calories 110
Protein 2 g
Carbohydrates 28 g
Fat 0 g
Saturated fat 0 g
Cholesterol 0 mg
Sodium 1 mg

ORANGE AND GRAPEFRUIT SEGMENTS

This is an attractive dish, especially if you use blood oranges, which contrast nicely with the grapefruit. In addition to using the flesh of the fruits, I mix the juice squeezed from the fruit membranes with a little honey to create a sauce. Garnished with mint and julienned orange skin, this makes a delightful dinner dessert with a slice of sponge cake or with cookies.

2   seedless navel or blood oranges
      (8 to 10 ounces each)
2   Ruby Red grapefruits (1 pound each)
2   tablespoons honey
      Mint leaves, for garnish
2   tablespoons julienned orange skin,
      for garnish

1. With a vegetable peeler, remove about six strips of peel from one of the oranges, and cut the strips into a fine julienne. Remove and discard the rest of the peel (including the white pith underneath) from the oranges and the grapefruits.

2. With a sharp knife, remove the orange and grapefruit segments from between their membranes, and then squeeze the membranes into a bowl to release the juices. (You should have 1 cup of combined juices.) Whisk the honey into the juice until combined.

3. Arrange alternating segments of orange and grapefruit in four dishes, and pour the sweetened juice over them. Garnish with mint leaves and julienned orange peel. Serve cold.

YIELD

4 servings

TOTAL TIME

About 20 minutes

NUTRITIONAL ANALYSIS PER SERVING

Calories 110

Protein 2 g

Carbohydrates 28 g

Fat 0 g

Saturated fat 0 g

Cholesterol 0 mg

Sodium 1 mg

GRAPES, RAISINS, DATES, FIGS, AND PRUNES

There are two types of grapes, those grown for table use and those grown for juice to make wine (more than a hundred varieties). ✑ Thompson Seedless grapes, oval in shape and smoky yellow in color, are probably the most common table variety. The Tokay Flame grape is large, round, and reddish and comes in smaller bunches than the Thompson. Concord grapes, occasionally available at the end of the summer, are thick-skinned, somewhat tart, and usually made into jelly. Their strong flavor reminds me of the wine made by our next-door neighbor when I was a child, using what are called Noah grapes in France. His wine had an awful taste and stained everything it touched, including your tongue and teeth. ✑ Ruby Red grapes, often available in full summer, are dark red with a thin skin. The Almeria is a greenish-yellow grape that is quite sweet, and the Muscat variety is deep yellow, fragrant, and very sweet. The Black Hamburg grape is very juicy and flavorful. ✑ Most grapes are sprayed with insecticides, so wash them before eating. Store them in the refrigerator, as they are perishable. Grapes are good both fresh and cooked. At the end of a meal in France, grapes are traditionally eaten with cheese, nuts, a piece of bread, and a glass of wine.

Raisins are dried grapes, and California is one of the greatest producers in the world of both golden and dark raisins. Thompson Seedless are most commonly used for raisins here. The dark raisins get brown when sun-dried for several weeks, while the golden raisins are treated with sulfur dioxide to keep them light. Zante grapes, sometimes

Grapes don't continue to ripen after they are picked and will only deteriorate after purchase.

95

referred to as champagne grapes, are used to make the small, dark raisins we call dried currants. Raisins are high in iron and potassium.

Dates grow in thick clusters on very large palm trees. Fresh dates, smooth, plump, and sometimes still hanging from their stems, are occasionally available in markets at the end of summer. They are delicious but not as sweet as the wrinkled dried dates, whose sugar is concentrated. ✎ Dried dates come individually wrapped and arranged in neat rows in packages or compressed into a "brick." They are usually used in pies or cakes. The dried dates commonly found in supermarkets are not as good as the large, plump specimens found in the markets in North Africa or Turkey. A fermented wine from dates is made in North Africa. ✎ Select the largest, softest dates, from golden to deep brown in color. Avoid any that have crystals of sugar on top, as they are too dry. To separate tightly packaged dates, it sometimes helps to soften them in a warm oven for a few minutes.

A member of the mulberry family, the fig is shaped like a small pear. Different types have skin colors from green to reddish-brown. They are high in iron and calcium. ✎ Figs were brought to this country by Spanish missionaries, which is why one California variety is called the Mission fig. The green-skinned Calimyrna fig is grown in California from the variety called Smyrna in Turkey. The small, firm Black Mission fig has a dark blue skin, is bright red inside, and has a concentrated taste, while Kadota and White Conadria figs are green outside and red inside. These are the varieties most common in American markets,

Raisins are extremely useful in desserts, garnishes, stuffings, chutneys, savory dishes, and more.

but more than a hundred varieties are found worldwide. ⌇ During school vacations, I spent time in the south of France at my godfather's house in Valence. He had a fig tree that yielded two crops each year, in June and September or October. Its figs, green outside and pink inside, are still my favorites. ⌇ Fresh figs are usually available from June to October in markets across the United States. They are excellent with prosciutto or as a garnish to a pâté, and they are also good baked or broiled. Fresh figs are very perishable. Choose only plump, unblemished ones. ⌇ Figs are also available canned in syrup or dried. I love dried figs and use them a great deal in my cooking, in chutneys, cakes, and other desserts. They combine well with anise and nuts.

Not all plums can become prunes. Prunes are a specific type of elongated, dark plum, which is left on the tree until it starts to shrivel; most other plums would spoil if left on the tree that long. ⌇ The great prune that I remember from my youth is the *pruneau d'Agen,* from the south of France. This variety is enormous, soft, and extremely flavorful. It tastes wonderful soaked in Armagnac, a liqueur from the same area. ⌇ Prunes go very well in any type of stuffing and complement rich meats, such as goose and pork. Best of all, in my estimation, are prunes stuffed with *foie gras* (goose liver pâté). ⌇ Prunes are usually packaged by size, from small to jumbo, pitted or unpitted. Refrigerated, the packages keep for months. Although this fruit is diuretic for some people and high in calories, it is a great source of fiber.

Select prunes that are slightly soft and shiny, with no evidence of crystallized sugar on them.

97

GRAPES, ORANGES, AND CURRANTS IN LIME COOKIE CONES

Here is an impressive, make-ahead dessert worthy of any occasion. A crisp, lime-flavored cookie is rolled into a cone and served with a simple mixture of grapes, oranges, the small raisins we know as currants, and orange juice. ⌁ It is important to use a heavy, nonstick cookie sheet for this recipe. Using the underside of a spoon, spread the batter out on the sheet or one lined with a nonstick baking mat until it is very, very thin. As the cookies emerge from the oven, wrap them immediately around a cone-shaped mold (or cone-shaped coated paper drinking cup) until they are firm. If they cool before you can shape them, rewarm them briefly in the oven to soften them before proceeding; otherwise, they will crack.

CONES

1   tablespoon unsalted butter, melted
1   tablespoon canola oil
1   egg white
½   teaspoon pure vanilla extract
1   teaspoon grated lime rind
3   tablespoons all-purpose flour
3   tablespoons granulated sugar

FILLING

2   oranges
2   cups seedless Red Flame grapes
     (about 10 ounces)
⅓   cup dried currants (small raisins)
2   tablespoons orange juice
2   tablespoons honey or maple syrup

     Confectioners' sugar, for decoration
     Mint leaves or edible flowers (optional)

FOR THE CONES

1. Preheat the oven to 375 degrees.

2. In a mixing bowl, whisk together the melted butter, oil, egg white, vanilla, lime rind, flour, and granulated sugar until smooth.

3. Spoon about 1 tablespoon of batter at four equally spaced intervals on a nonstick cookie sheet or aluminum cookie sheet lined with a nonstick baking mat or parchment paper. Using the back of a spoon, spread each mound of batter with a circular motion until it is very thin and extends to a diameter of at least 5 inches. Bake for 7 to 8 minutes, or until nicely browned (some areas will be browner than others).

4. Using a large spatula, immediately lift the cookies from the cookie sheet, and wrap them, one at a time, around a cone-shaped

(CONTINUED)

Grapes, Oranges, and Currants in Lime Cookie Cones (this page).

YIELD
4 servings

TOTAL TIME
About 45 minutes

———

NUTRITIONAL
ANALYSIS
PER SERVING
Calories 246
Protein 3 g
Carbohydrates 47 g
Fat 7 g
Saturated fat 2 g
Cholesterol 8 mg
Sodium 17 mg

metal mold. (Mine is 4 inches long and has an opening diameter of about 4 inches.) Alternatively, shape them into cones by hand. If the unrolled cookies become brittle, reheat them in the oven for about 30 seconds. Cool the cones on a rack. Repeat with the remaining batter. (You should have about eight cookies.)

FOR THE FILLING

5. Peel the oranges, removing the white pith and surrounding membrane from each. Halve the oranges lengthwise. With a paring knife, trim off the central core, and cut the flesh into 1-inch cubes. Cut the grapes in half. Mix the oranges, grapes, currants, orange juice, and honey in a bowl, and set the mixture aside until serving time.

6. To serve, arrange the cones on a serving platter, with their pointed tips extending beyond the edges. Spoon the fruit into the center of the platter, so that it appears to be emerging from the cones. Sprinkle with the confectioners' sugar, and garnish with the mint leaves or edible flowers, if desired. Serve two cones per person with about ½ cup of the fruit.

GRAPES AND RAISINS IN LEMON JUICE

In this simple dessert, grapes and raisins are marinated in sweetened lemon juice. I love the two contrasting textures in this combination: the seedless grapes provide crispness, the raisins chewiness.

YIELD
4 servings

TOTAL TIME
10 minutes

———

NUTRITIONAL
ANALYSIS
PER SERVING
Calories 211
Protein 2 g
Carbohydrates 56 g
Fat 0 g
Saturated fat 0 g
Cholesterol 0 mg
Sodium 6 mg

2   *tablespoons lemon juice*
⅓   *cup sugar*
2½ *cups white seedless grapes*
1   *cup dark raisins*

1. Mix the lemon juice and sugar together in a bowl large enough to hold the fruit.

2. Wash the grapes, and pat them dry with paper towels. Add the grapes and raisins to the bowl. Mix well, and serve immediately, or refrigerate for up to 4 hours.

3. Spoon into four wineglasses, and serve cold.

GRAPES IN RED WINE SAUCE

This is a refreshing summer dessert that looks most attractive served in stemmed glasses. Yogurt gives the dish an appealing look, and its acidity contrasts nicely with the sweetness of the grapes and accompanying wine sauce. It is essential that you use Red Flame grapes here. They can withstand cooking better than most other grape varieties. Although their skins will crack, they won't fall apart the way many other grapes do when cooked.

 Potato starch or flour is made from steamed potatoes that are then dried and ground. Gluten-free, it is often used as a thickener, as it is here, and sometimes appears in baked goods, particularly Jewish Passover specialties, in place of wheat flour. It can be found in the ethnic food sections of some supermarkets and in Asian specialty food shops (since it is also used in Japanese cooking). If potato starch in not available in your area, however, substitute the same amount of commercial dried instant mashed potatoes.

1 cup sturdy, fruity red wine
1½ pounds seedless Red Flame grapes (4 cups)
¼ cup currant jelly
¼ teaspoon ground cinnamon
2 teaspoons potato starch (potato flour)
1 cup plain yogurt

1. Reserve 1 tablespoon of the wine.

2. Place the grapes in a saucepan with the rest of the wine, the jelly, and the cinnamon. Bring the mixture to a boil, cover, reduce the heat to low, and boil gently for 4 to 5 minutes, or just until the grapes begin to crack open. Set the pan off the heat.

3. Dissolve the potato starch in the reserved tablespoon of wine, and stir it into the grape mixture.

4. Cool the dessert to room temperature, and serve it in stemmed glasses with a generous spoonful of yogurt.

YIELD
4 servings

TOTAL TIME
About 10 minutes, plus cooling time

NUTRITIONAL ANALYSIS PER SERVING
Calories 234
Protein 4 g
Carbohydrates 46 g
Fat 1 g
Saturated fat 1 g
Cholesterol 3 mg
Sodium 49 mg

PECAN-AND-ARMAGNAC-STUFFED DATES

These dates are an appealing dessert or a welcome snack at any hour of the day. I like to use the very large Medjool dates when they are available, but regular dates are fine for this recipe. The stuffing mixture is mostly cookies, of any type you have on hand.

YIELD

4 servings

TOTAL TIME

15 minutes

NUTRITIONAL ANALYSIS PER SERVING

Calories 282

Protein 3 g

Carbohydrates 51 g

Fat 8 g

Saturated fat 1 g

Cholesterol 0 mg

Sodium 209 mg

20 regular-size dried, pitted dates, or 12 very large Medjool pitted dates

3 ounces cookies (I use gingersnaps, but chocolate chip, tuiles, or even graham crackers can be substituted)

1½ tablespoons lemon juice

1½ tablespoons Armagnac or cognac (or orange juice, if you prefer a nonalcoholic version)

⅓ cup coarsely chopped pecans

1 tablespoon minced fresh mint

20 small spearmint or peppermint leaves, for decoration

1. Using a sharp knife, almost split the dates lengthwise, stopping before cutting them in half entirely, and open each one like a book.

2. Crush the cookies coarsely in a small bowl, and lightly mix in the lemon juice and Armagnac. Add the pecans and minced mint, and mix until the ingredients are well combined.

3. If you are using regular dates, spoon about 1 teaspoon of the cookie mixture into the center of each open date, and gently fold the date around it to partially enclose the stuffing. For Medjool dates, use about 2 teaspoons of the cookie mixture to fill each date.

4. Decorate the dates by inserting the stem end of a small mint leaf in the center of the stuffed edge. Arrange the dates on a platter, and refrigerate them until serving time.

Pecan-and-Armagnac-Stuffed Dates (this page).

BROILED FIGS IN PEACH SAUCE

Wait to do this dessert until ripe figs are available. The ripeness of the fruit determines the quality of the dish, as it does in most fruit desserts. The figs are halved, sprinkled with sugar, and then broiled to caramelize their tops. They are served with a mixture of peach preserves, lemon juice, and rum.

1   *pound ripe black figs (often called Mission figs)*
1½ *tablespoons sugar*

PEACH SAUCE

¼   *cup peach preserves*
2   *tablespoons lemon juice*
2   *tablespoons dark rum*

Clockwise from top: Pears in Grenadine (see page 141); Apricot Délice (see page 33); Broiled Figs in Peach Sauce (this page).

1. Preheat a broiler.

2. Cut the figs in half lengthwise, and arrange them cut side up in one layer in a gratin dish. Sprinkle them with the sugar.

3. Place the figs under the broiler about 3 inches from the heat for 5 to 6 minutes, or until they are slightly caramelized on top and soft when pierced with a fork. Set them aside to cool while you make the peach sauce.

4. In a small bowl, mix the peach preserves, lemon juice, and rum.

5. Spoon the sauce over the figs, and let them rest at room temperature until serving time. Serve the dessert at room temperature.

YIELD
4 servings

TOTAL TIME
About 20 minutes

NUTRITIONAL ANALYSIS PER SERVING
Calories 168
Protein 1 g
Carbohydrates 40 g
Fat 0 g
Saturated fat 0 g
Cholesterol 0 mg
Sodium 11 mg

CALIMYRNA FIGS IN SPICY PORT SAUCE

Calimyrna is a combined word used to describe a variety of figs grown in California but native to Smyrna, Turkey. When dried, these are pale yellow or beige and have thicker skins than Mission figs, which are jet black. Port wine complements the sweet intense flavor of the figs in this dessert. The sweetness of the wine, however, is lessened somewhat by the addition of delightfully bitter Campari and cayenne pepper. The poaching liquid around the fruit is thickened a little, and the figs are served with this natural sauce and yogurt, which is lower in calories than sour cream.

YIELD
6 servings

TOTAL TIME
About 30 minutes

———

NUTRITIONAL
ANALYSIS
PER SERVING
Calories 306
Protein 4 g
Carbohydrates 59 g
Fat 2 g
Saturated fat 1 g
Cholesterol 5 mg
Sodium 29 mg

1   pound dried Calimyrna figs (about 20)
1½ cups water
1   cup port
¼   cup Campari
    Dash cayenne pepper
1   teaspoon cornstarch dissolved in
    1 tablespoon water
1   cup plain yogurt

1. Stand the figs in a large saucepan, and add the water. Cover the pan, bring the water to a boil over high heat, then reduce the heat to low, and boil the figs gently for 5 minutes. Add the port, Campari, and cayenne. Bring the mixture back to a boil, cover, reduce the heat to low, and boil for another 5 minutes.

2. Stir in the dissolved cornstarch, mix well, and return the cooking liquid to a boil. Remove the pan from the heat, and cool the figs in the cooking liquid.

3. To serve, divide the yogurt among six serving plates, and spread it out in a circle. Arrange three or four figs on top of the yogurt on each plate, and spoon some cooking liquid over them. Serve.

FROZEN BLACK VELVET

Kahlua, figs, and chocolate-coated coffee beans bring this simple dessert to a high level of sophistication. Served in crystal goblets, it makes a terrific finish for an elegant meal. Ice cream can, of course, be substituted for the frozen yogurt if you are not counting calories. If you would rather not use alcohol, substitute a few drops of vanilla extract or strong coffee for the Kahlua. (See photograph, page 61.)

1 *pint good-quality nonfat vanilla frozen yogurt*
4 *tablespoons Kahlua or another coffee-flavored liqueur*
4 *dried figs, each cut into about 6 wedges*
12 *chocolate-coated coffee beans*

1. Divide the frozen yogurt among four dishes, and pour 1 tablespoon of the Kahlua over each serving. Arrange the fig wedges on top of and around the yogurt, and sprinkle on the coffee beans. Serve.

YIELD
4 servings

TOTAL TIME
5 minutes

———

NUTRITIONAL
ANALYSIS
PER SERVING
Calories 203
Protein 3 g
Carbohydrates 40 g
Fat 1 g
Saturated fat 1 g
Cholesterol 1 mg
Sodium 50 mg

FIGS VILAMOURA

Vilamoura is a town in the southern part of Portugal, where you can find dried figs prepared this way in the market. Use the largest dried figs that you can find for this presentation. The figs are partially split, spread out, and "sandwiched" together, with almonds inserted in the corners. The figs are then dried in an oven to concentrate their taste and brown the almonds. Very high in fiber, these go well with a glass of sweet port wine from Portugal, some Gorgonzola cheese, and a chunk of crusty bread.

YIELD

4 to 6 servings

TOTAL TIME

30 to 40 minutes

**NUTRITIONAL
ANALYSIS
PER SERVING
(6 SERVINGS)**

Calories 288

Protein 5 g

Carbohydrates 61 g

Fat 6 g

Saturated fat 1 g

Cholesterol 0 mg

Sodium 11 mg

1   *pound dried Mission (dark) figs
    (about 24)*

48 *whole unpeeled almonds*

1. Preheat the oven to 350 degrees.

2. Partially split the figs in half, starting at the base, but leave them attached at the stem end. Split each half in half again in the same way, and gently press the figs, skin side up, on the work surface. (They should look like flowers or four-leaf clovers with each "petal" or "leaf" still attached at the stem.)

3. When all the figs have been split and pressed, make a "sandwich" by pressing two figs together, flesh against flesh. Then push the almonds, rounded ends first, about one-third of the way into the figs where the "petals" connect near the stem, and press to ensure that the almonds are held securely.

4. Spread the fig "flowers" on a tray, and bake for 20 minutes to brown the almonds and dry the figs. (This concentrates their flavor.)

5. Let the figs cool, and store them in a tightly covered container until ready to serve. They will keep for up to 2 weeks.

PRUNES AND GRAPEFRUIT IN RED WINE SAUCE

This combination of cooked prunes and raw grapefruit in a red wine sauce has an appealingly tart taste and is very pleasing to the eye, although one of the fruits could be eliminated and the other served on its own in this manner also. Either way, this simple fruit dessert is a welcome ending to a rich meal.

½   *pound large pitted dried prunes (about 24)*
2   *tablespoons light brown sugar*
¾   *cup dry red wine*
1   *vanilla bean*
¼   *teaspoon black peppercorns*
4 to 6 *whole cloves*
2   *small Ruby Red grapefruits (about 1½ pounds)*

1. Place the prunes, sugar, wine, and vanilla bean in a saucepan.

2. Place the peppercorns and cloves on a small square of cheesecloth, and tie them into a package (for easy removal after cooking). Add the cheesecloth package to the saucepan, and bring the mixture to a boil. Cover, reduce the heat to low, and cook gently for 10 minutes.

3. Meanwhile, peel the grapefruits, removing the skin and the white pith underneath. With a sharp knife, remove the segments from between the membranes so the grapefruit flesh is entirely exposed. Squeeze the membranes over a bowl to release any remaining juice. Add about ⅓ cup of the juice to the prunes in the saucepan, and cool the mixture.

4. At serving time, remove and discard the cheesecloth package, and divide the prunes among four plates. Arrange about four grapefruit segments alongside the prunes on each plate. Pour the prune-cooking juices over the fruit, and serve.

YIELD
4 servings

TOTAL TIME
20 to 30 minutes

NUTRITIONAL ANALYSIS PER SERVING
Calories 220
Protein 2 g
Carbohydrates 50 g
Fat 0 g
Saturated fat 0 g
Cholesterol 0 mg
Sodium 7 mg

MANGOES

I remember seeing absolutely enormous mango trees in the Caribbean Islands. In the minds of many people, a ripe mango is the best-tasting fruit in the world. It is relatively low in calories, however—about 140 for a large one—and very high in vitamin A, vitamin C, and potassium.　　Ripe mangoes are a bit soft when you press on them, and their skin is very smooth. They have a sweet fragrant smell; underripe ones have virtually no smell, and overripe ones smell like turpentine. To preserve their aroma, don't cut the fruit until just before you use it. I like to halve mangoes lengthwise, cutting into them with a sharp knife on each side of the central pit. Then I scoop the fruit out of each half. This is one of the best ways to eat a mango. After that, I suck on the pit, which is a messy but delicious way of getting every last bit of the flesh.　　Mangoes marry particularly well with dark rum and cognac and are a prime ingredient in chutneys made in India and England. Besides the large mangoes available in markets, there are smaller green varieties, which are pickled or used in sauces and preserves. Combined with hot pepper, fish sauce, sugar, and coriander, shredded green mango makes one of the tastiest and most invigorating salads in Thailand.

When eaten out of hand, a mango makes a real mess, because this juicy delicacy tends to run.

ALMOND CAKE WITH MANGO *COULIS*

Colorful mango *coulis* (French for a liquid puree), flavored with rum and a bit of honey, is the perfect accompaniment to my favorite almond cake. Be sure to use only a very ripe mango for the *coulis*. For a more festive presentation, sprinkle sliced almonds on the cake batter just before baking. ✎ To make this traditional cake less caloric, I have drastically reduced the amount of butter and the number of egg yolks. Be sure to beat the egg whites until fairly firm and to fold them into the almond batter quickly enough so they don't have a chance to deflate. Folding should take only a few seconds with a spatula. Transfer the batter to the greased baking mold, and bake immediately.

YIELD

10 servings

TOTAL TIME

About 1 hour

———

NUTRITIONAL ANALYSIS PER SERVING

Calories 256

Protein 6 g

Carbohydrates 31 g

Fat 13 g

Saturated fat 2 g

Cholesterol 67 mg

Sodium 34 mg

ALMOND CAKE

3½ teaspoons canola oil

5½ ounces sliced almonds (1½ cups)

¾ cup sugar

¼ cup potato starch (see the introduction to Grapes in Red Wine Sauce on page 101)

1 tablespoon unsalted butter, softened

1 teaspoon pure vanilla extract

3 egg yolks

2 tablespoons milk

5 egg whites

MANGO *COULIS*

1 ripe mango (about 1 pound)

¼ cup water

2 tablespoons dark rum

1 tablespoon lemon juice

2 tablespoons honey

FOR THE ALMOND CAKE

1. Preheat the oven to 325 degrees.

2. Grease the bottom and sides of an 8-by-1-inch round mold with ½ teaspoon of the oil, and line the bottom of the mold with parchment paper.

3. Place the almonds, ¼ cup of the sugar, and the potato starch in the bowl of a food processor. Process until the nuts are finely ground. Add the butter, the remaining 3 teaspoons of oil, all but 2 tablespoons of the remaining sugar, the vanilla, the egg yolks, and the milk, and process just until the mixture is smooth. Transfer it to a bowl.

4. In another bowl, beat the egg whites until firm; then add the reserved 2 tablespoons of sugar, and beat for a few seconds longer.

5. Fold the egg white mixture quickly into the almond mixture, and transfer the batter to the greased mold. Bake for 35 minutes, or until set. Cool in the pan on a rack.

FOR THE MANGO *COULIS*

6. Cut the mango in half lengthwise, and scoop out the flesh. Place the flesh in the bowl of a food processor, and process it until smooth. Add the water, rum, lemon juice, and honey, and process until smooth.

7. To serve, unmold the cake, cut it into wedges, and serve it with the mango *coulis*.

MANGO SYMPHONY

After marinating in a honey–rum sauce, pieces of plum are spooned into the center of plates ringed with mango slices, and the remaining sauce is drizzled over both fruits. The result is a wonderfully complementary blend of flavors.

1   ripe mango (about 1 pound)
2   Santa Rosa or Black Friar plums (8 ounces)
3   tablespoons honey
2   tablespoons dark rum of best quality

1. Peel the mango, and slice it thinly, cutting all around the central pit. Discard the pit. Place the slices in a bowl, cover, and refrigerate until cold.

2. Meanwhile, halve the plums, discard the pits, and cut the flesh into ½-inch pieces.

(You should have about 2 cups.) Mix the honey and rum in a bowl large enough to hold the plums. Add the plum pieces, mix well, cover, and refrigerate until cold.

3. At serving time, arrange the slices of mango around the periphery of four dessert plates. Spoon the plums into the center of the plates and drizzle the remaining marinade from the plums over all the fruit. Serve immediately.

YIELD
4 servings

TOTAL TIME
15 minutes,
plus chilling time

———

**NUTRITIONAL
ANALYSIS
PER SERVING**
Calories 145
Protein 0 g
Carbohydrates 33 g
Fat 1 g
Saturated fat 0 g
Cholesterol 0 mg
Sodium 2 mg

SOUFFLÉ OF MANGO WITH MANGO SAUCE

The flesh of two ripe mangoes is pureed here, with half the puree strained to make a sauce and the remainder combined with beaten egg whites for the soufflé. Because there are no egg yolks in the base of this soufflé—it consists solely of mango puree and a little sugar—the assembled dish will keep, refrigerated, for a few hours before baking, provided the egg whites are well beaten and stiff. In fact, the unbaked soufflé can even be frozen for up to 2 weeks.

1	teaspoon unsalted butter
4	tablespoons granulated sugar
2	very ripe mangoes (about 1 pound each)
2	tablespoons grenadine syrup
2	tablespoons Grand Marnier liqueur
2	tablespoons water
3	egg whites
1	teaspoon confectioners' sugar
2	kiwis (about 3 ounces each), peeled and cut into ½-inch dice (⅔ cup)

1. If you will bake the soufflé immediately after preparing it, preheat the oven to 375 degrees.

2. Using the butter and 1 tablespoon of the granulated sugar, butter and sugar a 3½-to-4-cup soufflé mold.

3. Peel and pit the mangoes, and puree the flesh in a food processor. (You should have 2 cups.) Set 1 cup of the puree aside in a bowl large enough to hold the soufflé mixture. Strain the remaining cup of puree through a fine strainer set over a small bowl. (You should have about ¾ cup strained.)

4. Add the grenadine, Grand Marnier, and water to the strained puree, mix, cover, and refrigerate. (You should have about 1¼ cups of mango sauce.)

(CONTINUED)

YIELD
4 servings

TOTAL TIME
About 1 hour

———

NUTRITIONAL ANALYSIS PER SERVING
Calories 233
Protein 4 g
Carbohydrates 52 g
Fat 2 g
Saturated fat 1 g
Cholesterol 3 mg
Sodium 46 mg

Clockwise from right: Soufflé of Mango with Mango Sauce (this page); Cranberry Soufflés with Cranberry–Red Wine Sauce (see page 62); Mangoes with Cognac (see page 115).

5. Beat the egg whites by hand or with a mixer until stiff, then add the remaining 3 tablespoons of granulated sugar, and beat a few more seconds. Add about half of the beaten whites to the reserved cup of mango puree, and mix with a whisk. Then, working as quickly as you can, gently but thoroughly fold in the rest of the egg whites with a rubber spatula.

6. Fill the prepared mold with the soufflé mixture. Smooth the top, then decorate it with ridges or lines, if desired, using the blade of a knife or metal spatula, or mound the excess mixture in the center of the soufflé to create a decorative "knob" (see photograph, page 112).

Alternative serving of Soufflé of Mango with Mango Sauce (step 8 on this page).

7. If you are baking the soufflé immediately, place it in the preheated oven for about 25 minutes, or until it is puffed and golden on top. Alternatively, refrigerate the soufflé, uncovered, for up to an hour, and then bake it; or freeze it, uncovered, for at least 12 hours until solid, then cover it with plastic wrap (which won't stick to the frozen soufflé), and freeze for up to 2 weeks. Remove the soufflé from the freezer 1 hour before baking, immediately peel off the plastic wrap, and let the soufflé sit at room temperature to defrost partially. Then preheat the oven to 350 degrees, and bake the soufflé for 25 to 35 minutes, until it is puffed, golden, and set.

8. Sprinkle the hot soufflé with the confectioners' sugar. Divide the sauce among four dessert plates, and sprinkle the diced kiwi on top. Bring the soufflé to the table, and serve large spoonfuls of it on top of the sauce. Alternatively, let the soufflé cool to room temperature. (It will deflate to about the level of the uncooked mixture in the mold.) Cover with plastic wrap, and refrigerate until ready to serve. At serving time, unmold onto a platter, cut into wedges, and serve with the mango sauce.

MANGOES WITH COGNAC

This simple but elegant mango and cognac dessert is a sure winner, provided it is made with ripe fruit. Mangoes are available year-round now, but are usually of better quality at summer's end. ⌒ If you have any of the dessert left over, puree it in a food processor, and spread it on toast for breakfast the following morning. (See photograph, page 112.)

2   *ripe mangoes (about 12 ounces each)*
2   *to 3 strips lime peel (green part only),*
    removed with a vegetable peeler or zester
3   *tablespoons sugar*
2   *tablespoons cognac, rum, or whiskey*
3   *tablespoons lime juice*

1. Peel the mangoes, cutting deeply enough into the fruit so that any green-colored flesh is also removed. Then cut each mango inward, toward the pit, to make slices about ½ inch thick. Discard the pits.

2. Stack the lime peel strips, and cut them into thin julienne "sticks." (You should have about 1 tablespoon of julienned peel.)

3. In a bowl, combine the mango slices with the sugar, cognac, and lime juice.

4. Either serve immediately, or, for added flavor, chill for at least 2 hours, stirring occasionally. Serve in chilled goblets or glass bowls, sprinkled with the julienned peel.

YIELD
4 servings

TOTAL TIME
10 minutes,
plus chilling time
(optional)

NUTRITIONAL ANALYSIS PER SERVING
Calories 134
Protein 1 g
Carbohydrates 30 g
Fat 0 g
Saturated fat 0 g
Cholesterol 0 mg
Sodium 4 mg

MELONS

I remember with fondness the small *cavaillon* melons that my mother used to serve at her restaurant. Named for a small town in the south of France, this aromatic melon with deep-orange flesh is often served with port wine as the first course of a dinner. ↝ The variety of melons at the market nowadays is amazing. The most common is probably the cantaloupe, which reaches its peak in full summer. The blossom end of the ripe fruit will yield slightly to a little pressure, and the stem area will have a fragrant smell. In France we have a smaller variety called the Charentais. ↝ The casaba melon has a golden-yellow skin and pale-green flesh. It is very juicy and has a distinctive taste. The crenshaw, with pale-pink flesh, has skin that is initially dark green but becomes almost yellow as it ripens. Honeydew, part of the muskmelon family, has smooth, pale, greenish-white skin and pale-green flesh. Less common melons include the pepino, which is small, about the size of a papaya, and the Canary, which has a brilliant yellow skin and very white flesh, and tastes, to me, a little like pineapple. ↝ The watermelon, a favorite of children and adults alike in summer, is related to the cucumber and is thought to have originated in Africa. Some watermelons weigh as much as 30 pounds. Common varieties have deep-green skin, which

Cantaloupes should be picked ripe; if picked earlier, they never achieve full flavor.

is sometimes marbled, deep red flesh, and black seeds. A newer seedless variety has far fewer, softer seeds. ❧ Melons make good sherbets and great first courses with prosciutto. They have a low calorie count, although, strangely enough, watermelon has almost twice the calories of cantaloupe or honeydew, about 68 to a pound. Melons are high in iron, potassium, and vitamins A and C.

FROZEN WATERMELON SLUSH

Although I love watermelon, when I eat it in conventional slices, I find its seeds troublesome. Here, the seeds are removed, and the flesh is pureed and frozen solid. A few hours before it is to be served, the mixture is transferred to the refrigerator to soften; then it is broken into flakes or shavings and spooned into glass goblets or bowls. Delicious and refreshing, it is the perfect dessert on a hot day.

1   *medium watermelon (about 12 pounds)*
¾   *cup lime or lemon juice*
¾   *cup sugar*

Frozen Watermelon Slush (this page).

1. Cut the watermelon into 2-inch wedges. Remove and discard the rind, black seeds, and as many of the softer white seeds as possible. Cut the flesh into 1-inch chunks, and place them in the bowl of a food processor. Process until liquefied, although some small chunks may remain. (You will have about 10 cups.) Add the lime or lemon juice and sugar, and process just until they are incorporated.

2. Transfer the mixture to a stainless steel bowl, cover, and freeze until solid, for 8 to 10 hours.

3. At least 3 to 4 hours (but as long as 5 hours) before serving, move the bowl to the refrigerator to soften the mixture. In the last hour before serving, use a fork to break the softened mixture into shavings. Serve the slush in cold glass goblets or bowls.

YIELD
8 servings

TOTAL TIME
About 30 minutes, plus 12 to 14 hours' freezing and softening time

---

NUTRITIONAL
ANALYSIS
PER SERVING
Calories 210
Protein 3 g
Carbohydrates 50 g
Fat 2 g
Saturated fat 0 g
Cholesterol 0 mg
Sodium 12 mg

FRAGRANT MELON SOUP

This soup gives you an opportunity to experiment with different melons. Although melons with orange-colored flesh produce the most attractive result, the recipe will work with almost any ripe variety. The tangerine juice can be replaced with orange juice, and the cardamom seeds can be omitted, if unavailable.

YIELD

4 servings

TOTAL TIME

About 30 minutes, plus cooling time

———

NUTRITIONAL ANALYSIS PER SERVING

Calories 177

Protein 2 g

Carbohydrates 37 g

Fat 1 g

Saturated fat 0 g

Cholesterol 0 mg

Sodium 16 mg

12 cardamom pods
1   cup tangerine juice
¾   cup soft, mellow white wine
    (a Chenin Blanc, such as a Vouvray)
⅓   cup sugar
½   cup water
6   whole cloves
1   stick cinnamon, about 3 inches,
    broken into pieces
1   tablespoon lime juice
1   tablespoon lime zest strips
½   teaspoon cornstarch dissolved in
    1 tablespoon water
1   ripe melon (about 2 pounds), peeled,
    seeded, and cut into 1-inch pieces
½   cup blueberries, for garnish
    Cookies or pound cake (optional)

1. Smash the cardamom pods with the base of a heavy saucepan, and retrieve the tiny black seeds inside. (You should have ½ teaspoon.)

2. Combine the cardamom seeds, tangerine juice, wine, sugar, water, cloves, cinnamon pieces, lime juice, and lime zest in a saucepan, preferably stainless steel. Bring the mixture to a boil, then reduce the heat to low, cover, and cook for about 15 minutes. Add the dissolved cornstarch and mix well. (You should have about 1¾ cups.) Add the melon to the hot soup, mix it in gently, and set it aside to cool.

3. Remove the cloves and cinnamon stick pieces, and serve the soup at room temperature or slightly cooler (but not ice cold) in deep plates with a sprinkling of blueberries on top. A few cookies or a slice of pound cake makes a nice accompaniment.

Fragrant Melon Soup (this page).

CANTALOUPE SHERBET

⌇

I peel a well-ripened, fragrant cantaloupe for this recipe and retain four crosswise slices for serving. The remainder is processed with sugar and lime juice and, eventually, transformed into a sherbet in an ice-cream maker. I serve the sherbet on top of the melon slices, which have been flavored with a little port wine and grenadine.

YIELD

4 servings

TOTAL TIME

About 20 minutes, plus churning time

———

NUTRITIONAL ANALYSIS PER SERVING

Calories 261

Protein 2 g

Carbohydrates 63 g

Fat 1 g

Saturated fat 0 g

Cholesterol 0 mg

Sodium 32 mg

1   ripe cantaloupe (about 3 pounds)
¼   cup port
4   tablespoons grenadine syrup
2   limes
½   cup sugar
     Edible flowers or herbs, for decoration
     (optional)

1. Using a sharp paring knife, peel the cantaloupe, removing the outer skin and green parts underneath so that the orange flesh is visible. Cut the melon in half crosswise, and, using a spoon, remove and discard the seeds. Cut four thin (¼-inch) crosswise slices from one of the melon halves to create four "wheels" or "rings," (about 6 ounces total). Place these rings in a gratin dish with the port and 2 tablespoons of the grenadine, cover, and set aside. Cut the rest of the melon into 1-inch pieces. (You should have about 5 cups.)

2. Using a lemon zester, remove enough thin strips of rind from one of the limes to measure 1 teaspoon. Set the strips aside. Halve and squeeze the limes to obtain 3 tablespoons of lime juice.

3. Place the melon pieces in the bowl of a food processor with the lime juice, sugar, and remaining 2 tablespoons of grenadine, and process until smooth. (You will have about 4 cups.)

4. Transfer the pureed melon mixture to an ice-cream maker, and process according to the manufacturer's instructions, churning the mixture for 25 to 30 minutes, until it is solid.

5. Serve immediately, or transfer the sherbet to cold containers, and store it in the freezer. If you are freezing the sherbet for later use, move it from the freezer to the refrigerator about 1½ hours before serving time to soften.

6. At serving time, arrange a melon ring (whole or in pieces) on each of four plates, and pour the accumulated juice in the gratin dish on top of and around the rings. Place a scoop of the sherbet in the center of each ring, and sprinkle a few of the reserved strips of lime rind on top. Decorate the sherbet with an edible flower or herb, if desired, and serve immediately.

CANTALOUPE AND STRAWBERRIES IN HONEY SAUCE

When selecting cantaloupes, your nose is the best indicator of ripeness. Choose a melon with a sweet, fruity fragrance.

¼   cup honey

1   tablespoon grated orange rind

2 to 3 tablespoons orange juice

1   tablespoon Grand Marnier liqueur

1   large cantaloupe (about 1½ pounds), seeded, peeled, and cut into 1-inch pieces (2½ cups)

1   cup strawberries, hulled, and halved or quartered, depending on size

1. Combine the honey, orange rind, orange juice, and Grand Marnier in a bowl large enough to hold the melon and strawberries. Add both fruits, and toss thoroughly.

2. Refrigerate until serving time. (This dessert can be assembled up to 6 hours ahead.)

3. At serving time, divide the fruit mixture among four goblets.

YIELD
4 servings

TOTAL TIME
15 minutes,
plus chilling time

NUTRITIONAL
ANALYSIS
PER SERVING
Calories 107
Protein 1 g
Carbohydrates 28 g
Fat 0 g
Saturated fat 0 gm
Cholesterol 0 mg
Sodium 9 mg

PEACHES AND NECTARINES

The peach is often called the queen of fruit and is the third most important fruit, after the apple and the banana, in American markets. The peaches available in markets (from May to October) are usually freestones, whose flesh is easily separated from their pits. There are over a thousand peach varieties. White peaches have appeared in the last few years; their flesh has a pink blush, and their skin is fuzzy and velvety. The most common peach is the Georgia Elberta, which has beautiful golden-yellow flesh. Other common varieties are the Red Heaven, the Loring, the Washington, and the Jersey Queen. Markets, however, usually label peaches merely as yellow or white, without giving varietal names. ⌖ The peak season for peaches is July and August, but dried, canned, and frozen peach segments, which are quite good, are available year-round. I look for fresh peaches with a deep reddish skin color and a soft interior, so I know they are ripe and ready to be used right away. I keep them at room temperature and eat them as they ripen. White peaches come to my market in late summer, and I always watch for them. They are more delicate than the yellow ones, bruise easily, and are more difficult to cook, yet their flavor is exquisite. I have a white peach tree at the back of my property and look forward to

For the Chinese,

who adore peaches,

the peach blossom

symbolizes

long life.

eating its fruit in the summer. ❧ Peaches are low in calories—only 38 to 40 in a large one—and high in calcium, potassium, and vitamin A. Don't eat peaches ice cold; they taste much better at room temperature. Most people peel peaches because they don't like the fuzzy skin. A firm peach can be peeled with a vegetable peeler; submerge a riper, softer peach in boiling water for a few seconds, and the skin will slide off easily. Nothing compares with eating a ripe peach right off the tree, still lukewarm from the sun.

The nectarine is a cross between a peach and a plum and has a smooth skin. It can be substituted for a peach in most recipes. In France it is called a *brugnon*. Nectarines have a longer market season than peaches, but the peak is still July and August. The most common variety sold is the LeGrand. ❧ It's not necessary to peel nectarines. They have more calories than peaches (about 70 in a large one), are fairly high in vitamins A and C, and are a good source of fiber.

Buy nectarines that yield to the touch a bit, and store them at room temperature.

BAKED PEACHES WITH ALMONDS

This is an easy dish to prepare. Unpeeled peaches are pitted, and then the peach halves are baked with a little maple syrup, brown sugar, butter, and almonds in a gratin dish. Excellent served at room temperature with the surrounding juice, the dessert is also good—if you want to splurge—with a sour cream garnish.

4   *ripe, firm peaches (1½ pounds)*
2   *cups water*
¼   *cup maple syrup*
1½ *tablespoons light brown sugar*
1   *tablespoon unsalted butter, broken into pieces*
⅓   *cup whole unblanched almonds*
    Sour cream (optional)

1. Preheat the oven to 350 degrees.

2. Using a sharp paring knife, cut the unpeeled peaches in half lengthwise, and remove the pits. Arrange the peaches cut side down in one layer in a gratin dish. Sprinkle the water, maple syrup, brown sugar, butter, and almonds on top of them.

3. Place the gratin dish on a cookie sheet, and bake the gratin for 40 minutes. Turn the peach halves so they are skin side down, and cook them for another 15 minutes. (At this point, the juice around the peaches should be syrupy.)

4. Turn the peaches carefully in the syrup so they are skin side up again, and cool them to room temperature. Serve two peach halves per person with some of the syrup and a little sour cream if desired.

YIELD

4 servings

TOTAL TIME

About 1 hour, plus cooling time

———

NUTRITIONAL
ANALYSIS
PER SERVING

Calories 199

Protein 3 g

Carbohydrates 30 g

Fat 9 g

Saturated fat 2 g

Cholesterol 8 mg

Sodium 127 mg

OEUFS À LA NEIGE IN PEACH SAUCE

A classic French dessert, *oeufs à la neige,* or snow eggs, consists of egg-shaped portions of meringue dropped into hot water and cooked briefly on top of the stove. I serve the snow eggs with a sauce made of canned peaches pureed with yogurt, a little sugar, Cointreau, and vanilla. Although similar in color and consistency to crème anglaise, the rich custard sauce traditionally served with the "eggs," my version is much less caloric. ⌣ The snow eggs may be finished in the conventional manner, with a drizzle of caramel on top, or, for a more dramatic effect, with strands of caramel angel hair. "Spinning" these golden threads of sugar is a sometimes tricky, often messy proposition, best suited to the more adventurous. Try adding a bit of beeswax to the hot caramel (a trick I learned from my good friend and fellow chef Jean-Claude Szurdak). The wax coats the sugar threads, making them less likely to stick together. Don't try this in hot, humid weather.

PEACH SAUCE

- ¾ cup nonfat plain yogurt
- ¾ cup sliced canned peaches in syrup
- 1½ tablespoons sugar
- 1½ tablespoons Cointreau or Grand Marnier liqueur
- ½ teaspoon pure vanilla extract

SNOW EGGS

- 3 large egg whites
- ¼ cup sugar

CARAMEL

- 3 tablespoons sugar
- 1 tablespoon water

ANGEL HAIR (ALTERNATIVE TOPPING)

- 1 cup sugar
- ¼ cup water
- 2 teaspoons grated edible wax, such as beeswax

FOR THE PEACH SAUCE

1. Place all the sauce ingredients in a blender or food processor, and process until smooth and foamy. If desired, strain the peach sauce through a fine-mesh strainer set over a bowl.

(CONTINUED)

Oeufs à la Neige *in Peach Sauce (this page), with both caramel and angel hair garnishes.*

TOTAL TIME

35 to 40 minutes with caramel topping; about 1 hour with angel hair topping

NUTRITIONAL ANALYSIS PER SERVING

Calories 192

Protein 5 g

Carbohydrates 41 g

Fat 0 g

Saturated fat 0 g

Cholesterol 1 mg

Sodium 77 mg

For the Snow Eggs

2. Bring about 6 cups of water to a boil in a large saucepan. Meanwhile, beat the egg whites in a mixer until they are firm (3 to 4 minutes). Add the ¼ cup of sugar, and continue beating at medium to high speed for 30 seconds. At this point, reduce the heat of the water so that it is no more than 180 degrees (just under the simmer/boil).

3. Using a ladle or a large spoon, scoop out four mounds of meringue one at a time, and, using another spoon, slide them into the hot (not boiling) water. Poach the egg white mounds for about 2½ minutes, then gently turn them over with a skimmer, and poach them for another 2½ minutes. Lift them carefully from the water, and drain them on paper towels.

For the Caramel

4. Not more than 3 hours before serving the snow eggs, place the caramel ingredients in a small, unlined copper or stainless steel saucepan. Mix just enough to combine them, then bring the mixture to a boil over high heat. Reduce the heat to medium, and continue boiling the mixture for about 3 minutes, until it thickens into a syrup and turns a rich caramel color. Take care that it doesn't burn.

5. While the caramel is cooking, pour the peach sauce into a serving dish or shallow glass bowl, and arrange the snow eggs on top in one layer. Remove the caramel from the stove, and immediately pour it directly on top of the snow eggs, dividing it equally among them. Serve, preferably within an hour.

For the Angel Hair (Alternative Topping)

6. Combine the 1 cup of sugar and ¼ cup of water in a small saucepan, bring to a boil over medium heat, and cook until a light ivory in color (about 335 degrees). Remove from the heat, and stir in the wax.

7. Cover the floor surrounding your work table with newspapers, and secure a long-handled spatula or wooden spoon so that the entire handle extends beyond the edge of the table.

8. When the syrup has cooled for a few minutes, hold two forks side by side in one hand (or use a small whisk with the wires clipped off where they begin to curve), and dip the tines into the pan. Lift some syrup, and wave the forks high over the spatula so that the dripping threads solidify in the air before falling over the extended handle.

9. Slide the collected strands off the handle, and use immediately to garnish the snow eggs, or store the strands in an airtight container for later use.

PEACHES IN RED WINE

In full summer, when peaches are ripe, soft, and juicy, this is one of my favorite desserts. I prepare it here with a little black currant liqueur and red wine, but the recipe can be made with white wine and a little honey or with champagne and a dash of *framboise* (raspberry brandy). When fresh peaches are not available, substitute a like amount of unsweetened individually quick-frozen (IQF) peaches. Be sure to defrost them first slowly in the refrigerator overnight.

4   *ripe yellow peaches (about 1½ pounds)*
3   *tablespoons sugar*
3   *tablespoons cassis (black currant liqueur)*
½   *cup fruity, acidic red wine, such as Beaujolais or Zinfandel*
4   *sprigs fresh mint*

1. Peel the peaches with a vegetable peeler, and cut each one into six wedges, discarding the pits and skin. (You should have about 3 cups of peach wedges.)

2. Place the peaches in a bowl with the sugar, cassis, and wine. Mix well, and refrigerate for at least an hour and as long as 8 hours.

3. To serve, divide the peaches and surrounding juice among four wine goblets. Top each dessert with a mint sprig.

YIELD
4 servings

TOTAL TIME
15 minutes,
plus chilling time

NUTRITIONAL ANALYSIS PER SERVING
Calories 159
Protein 1 g
Carbohydrates 30 g
Fat 0 g
Saturated fat 0 g
Cholesterol 0 mg
Sodium 3 mg

PEACH AND WALNUT TART

Peaches, one of my favorite fruits, are baked here in a tart shell created from dough containing a minimum of flour and butter. To absorb some of the peach juices and lend added flavor to the tart, the shell and the peaches are sprinkled before baking with a mixture of walnuts, flour, and sugar, ground together with the dough trimmings into a powder. The baked dessert is glazed, while still lukewarm, with a coating of jam and served at room temperature.

TART DOUGH

⅔   *cup all-purpose flour*
2   *tablespoons unsalted butter*
1   *tablespoon corn oil*
⅛   *teaspoon salt*
½   *teaspoon sugar*
1   *tablespoon cold water*

WALNUT MIXTURE

¼   *cup walnut pieces*
1   *tablespoon all-purpose flour*
1   *tablespoon sugar*

3 to 4 *ripe white or yellow peaches (about 1 pound), cut into quarters*
¼   *cup apricot preserves*

1. Preheat the oven to 400 degrees.

2. Place all the dough ingredients except the water in the bowl of a food processor. Process for about 15 seconds, or just until the mixture looks sandy. Add the water, and process for another 5 seconds, or just until the mixture begins to gather together. Transfer the dough to a piece of plastic wrap, and, using the wrap, gather the dough into a ball. Roll the dough between two sheets of plastic wrap until it is about 10 inches in diameter (it will be very thin). Place an 8-inch metal flan ring or removable-bottom quiche or tart pan on a cookie sheet, and fit the dough inside the ring, pressing it into place. Run the rolling pin over the top edge to remove any excess dough, and reserve the trimmings in the bowl of the food processor.

3. Add all the walnut mixture ingredients to the dough trimmings, and process until well combined.

(CONTINUED)

Left: *Peach and Walnut Tart (this page); right: Baked Stuffed Nectarines (see page 137).*

YIELD
6 servings

TOTAL TIME
About 1½ hours

NUTRITIONAL ANALYSIS PER SERVING
Calories 208
Protein 3 g
Carbohydrates 30 g
Fat 9 g
Saturated fat 3 g
Cholesterol 11 mg
Sodium 53 mg

4. Spread half of the walnut mixture on the bottom of the tart shell. Arrange ten of the peach quarters in one layer skin side down around the circumference of the shell. Cut the two remaining peach quarters in half and arrange them skin side up in the middle of the tart shell. Sprinkle the rest of the walnut mixture evenly on top.

5. Bake the tart for 1 hour. Cool to lukewarm on a cooling rack, and then, using a spoon, spread the apricot preserves carefully over the top. Remove the ring from around the tart (the dough will shrink enough in baking to allow easy removal).

6. Using two large hamburger spatulas, transfer the tart to a serving plate. Cut it into six wedges, and serve it at room temperature. Refrigerate any leftovers, and enjoy them the next day.

COOKED PEACHES IN SWEET WINE

This is an easy, refreshing summer dessert, particularly delicious at the peak of the peach season, when the fruit is plentiful, inexpensive, and most nutritious.

YIELD

4 servings

TOTAL TIME

About 20 minutes, plus cooling time

———

NUTRITIONAL
ANALYSIS
PER SERVING

Calories 239

Protein 2 g

Carbohydrates 44 g

Fat 0 g

Saturated fat 0 g

Cholesterol 0 mg

Sodium 5 mg

3 *large, slightly underripe peaches, peeled with a vegetable peeler and cut into ½-inch slices (4 cups)*

¼ *cup sugar*

2 *tablespoons fresh lemon juice*

¼ *cup water*

1 *cup sweet white wine (such as Sauternes, Beaumes-de-Venise, or vin de Glacière)*

4 *sprigs mint*

1. Place the peach slices, sugar, lemon juice, and water in a stainless steel saucepan, and bring the mixture to a boil over high heat. Cover, reduce the heat to low, and boil the peaches gently for 5 minutes, or until they are tender (but not falling apart) when pierced with the point of a sharp knife. Cool. (You should have 2½ cups.)

2. At serving time, stir the wine into the peaches. Divide the mixture among four glass goblets, and decorate each dessert with a sprig of mint. For a more dramatic presentation, add the wine to the goblets at the table.

PINWHEELS OF PEACHES WITH STRAWBERRY *COULIS*

This refreshing dessert is a favorite of mine in August, when peaches are plentiful, ripe, and inexpensive. If you use both white and yellow peaches, you can alternate segments of different colors to create a pinwheel effect on the plates. The contrasting colors of the peaches and the *coulis* make this festive dessert the perfect ending for an elegant menu.

1   *large lemon*
6   *large peaches, 3 white and 3 yellow
    (or all one color, if preferred), about
    8 ounces each (3 pounds total)
    Sugar to taste (optional)*
1   *pound strawberries*
1   *jar (12 ounces) strawberry preserves
    (1⅓ cups)*
1   *tablespoon kirsch*

1. Grate the lemon skin to obtain 2 teaspoons of zest, then halve the lemon, and squeeze the halves to obtain 3 tablespoons of juice. Place the zest and juice together in a bowl.

2. If the peaches are firm, peel them with a vegetable peeler to remove the skin; otherwise, peel them with a sharp paring knife. Cut each peach into eight segments, and mix the segments carefully with the lemon juice mixture. Add sugar, based on your taste preferences and the ripeness of the peaches; if the peaches are ripe and sweet, no sugar is needed.

3. Wash the strawberries, and hull them. Cut the berries in half crosswise, then cut enough of the ripe berry tips into ½-inch pieces to obtain about 1¾ cups, and place these in a bowl. Put the remaining berries (about 2 cups) in the bowl of a food processor with the preserves. Process the mixture until smooth, then pour it over the berry pieces in the bowl. Stir in the kirsch, and refrigerate.

4. At serving time, divide the berry *coulis* among six dessert plates. Arrange eight peach segments, the equivalent of one peach, on each plate, and spoon some of the surrounding juice from the peaches on top. Serve.

YIELD

6 servings

TOTAL TIME

About 30 minutes, plus chilling time

NUTRITIONAL ANALYSIS PER SERVING

Calories 251

Protein 2 g

Carbohydrates 64 g

Fat 1 g

Saturated fat 0 g

Cholesterol 0 mg

Sodium 24 mg

NECTARINE CRISP

For this recipe, you can use regular nectarines, the white-fleshed nectarines found in farm markets during the summer, or even peaches. As always, ripe fruit gives the best result; for less ripe and sweet fruit, add a little sugar to the fruit mixture.

YIELD
4 servings

TOTAL TIME
About 1 hour

———

NUTRITIONAL ANALYSIS PER SERVING
Calories 378
Protein 7 g
Carbohydrates 63 g
Fat 13 g
Saturated fat 7 g
Cholesterol 33 mg
Sodium 307 mg

¼ cup peach preserves
2 tablespoons lemon juice
1½ pounds ripe nectarines
    (3 to 4 nectarines)

DOUGH

⅔ cup all-purpose flour
⅓ cup old-fashioned oatmeal
3 tablespoons cold unsalted butter,
    cut into 1-inch pieces
2 tablespoons sugar
¼ teaspoon cinnamon
1 teaspoon baking powder
¼ teaspoon salt
1 tablespoon milk

½ cup sour cream (optional)

1. Preheat the oven to 375 degrees.

2. Mix the preserves and lemon juice together in a bowl. Cut each of the unpeeled nectarines into eight wedges, and combine them with the preserve mixture. Transfer the mixture to a gratin dish large enough to hold the nectarines in one layer.

3. Place all the dough ingredients except the milk in the bowl of a food processor, and process the mixture for 5 to 10 seconds. Add the milk, and process for another 5 seconds. The dough mixture should be mealy at this point. Arrange it evenly on top of the nectarines.

4. Place the gratin dish on a cookie sheet, and bake the dessert for 45 minutes, or until the fruit is soft and the topping nicely browned. Serve lukewarm with a garnish of sour cream, if desired.

BAKED STUFFED NECTARINES

The nectarine is used too seldom, even though it has a great taste and a firm texture that lends itself to many preparations. Here I stuff and bake halved nectarines. The stuffing, composed primarily of dried fruits, nuts, and graham crackers, can be changed to accommodate what you have available and your taste preferences. Increase or decrease the cooking time, depending on the ripeness of the fruit. (See photograph, page 132.)

STUFFING

2 tablespoons golden raisins
⅓ cup light brown sugar
2 tablespoons diced dried apricots
2 tablespoons chopped of pecans
   (¼-inch pieces)
1 tablespoon sour cream
¼ cup coarsely crushed graham crackers
¼ teaspoon cinnamon

3 very large, firm nectarines (1½ pounds)
⅓ cup water

SYRUP

2 tablespoons granulated white sugar
1 tablespoon water
2 tablespoons fresh lemon juice

1. Preheat the oven to 375 degrees.

2. Place all the ingredients for the stuffing in a bowl, and mix them together lightly. (The consistency should be loose and fluffy, not pasty.)

3. Halve the nectarines, and remove the pits. Cut a small slice from the skin side of each nectarine half so that it will sit flat with the hollow side up.

4. Pile some stuffing into the cavity of each nectarine, and arrange the stuffed nectarines side by side in a gratin dish. Pour the ⅓ cup of water around the nectarines in the dish. Bake the nectarines for about 20 minutes or until they are soft and lightly browned. Let them cool to lukewarm or room temperature.

5. Meanwhile, prepare the syrup: mix the sugar, the 1 tablespoon of water, and the lemon juice together until the sugar is dissolved. Spoon some of the syrup on top of and around the nectarines, and serve.

YIELD
4 to 6 servings

TOTAL TIME
About 30 minutes, plus cooling time

———

NUTRITIONAL
ANALYSIS
PER SERVING
(6 SERVINGS)
Calories 163
Protein 2 g
Carbohydrates 36 g
Fat 3 g
Saturated fat 1 g
Cholesterol 1 mg
Sodium 18 mg

PEARS

In France, pears are the king of fruits. Grown in temperate climates, they should be picked while still quite firm and not yet ripe; if left to ripen on the tree, they get mushy. They improve in flavor and texture when stored in a cool place or at room temperature for a few days. A ripe pear will yield to gentle pressure and have a wonderful aroma. Within a day or so, however, a pear can go from unripe to rotten. If you are lucky enough to have a pear tree, you can pick the fruit well before it is ripe and keep it in a cool cellar for up to a month, to use in tarts and other desserts. ❧ One variety of pears is quite different from another. A ripe Anjou or Bartlett may cook in only 5 minutes, while a Seckel or Bosc may take an hour. The Comice pear, considered by some the best for eating fresh, is very delicate but cooks quite well, holding its shape and maintaining its creamy interior. The Bosc is excellent for poaching and does not fall apart when cooked. ❧ Peeled pears tend to darken, so you should rub them with lemon juice or keep them in a mixture of lemon juice and water until they are cooked. Once cooked in a syrup, they will sink into the liquid and not discolor. ❧ Pears range from 80 to 120 calories and are a good source of fiber.

The varieties

of pears

number in

the thousands.

TENDER PEARS IN CARAMEL SAUCE

This is a wonderful recipe to make ahead, because it keeps well in the refrigerator for a week. Half a pear per person is sufficient, since the velvety sauce served with the pears makes the dessert quite rich and filling. You may serve it with cookies or a piece of brioche. (See photograph, page 143.)

YIELD
4 servings

TOTAL TIME
30 to 40 minutes, plus cooling time

NUTRITIONAL ANALYSIS PER SERVING
Calories 292
Protein 2 g
Carbohydrates 38 g
Fat 16 g
Saturated fat 9 g
Cholesterol 54 mg
Sodium 15 mg

2   *large, ripe but firm pears, preferably Bosc (8 to 10 ounces each)*
1   *tablespoon lemon juice*
1   *teaspoon pure vanilla extract*
⅓   *cup sugar*
1¼   *cups water*
⅔   *cup heavy cream*
1   *tablespoon pear brandy (optional)*
1   *tablespoon crushed pistachio nuts*
    Cookies or brioche (optional)

1. Peel the pears, halve them vertically, and core them. Arrange the pear halves cut side down in one layer in a large skillet, preferably stainless steel.

2. Add the lemon juice, vanilla, sugar, and water to the skillet, and bring the mixture to a boil. Reduce the heat to medium-high, cover, and cook until the pears are tender when pierced with the point of a sharp knife. (*Note:* The cooking time can range from 5 to 30 minutes, depending on the type and ripeness of the pears used. If a long cooking time is required and most of the liquid around the pears has evaporated, add water as needed.)

3. Transfer the cooked pears to a gratin dish, and reduce the liquid in the skillet by cooking it over high heat; it will turn syrupy initially, then become a thick, brown caramel.

4. Add the cream, pouring it in a little at a time so that it doesn't splatter. Mix well with a whisk or spoon, then bring the mixture back to a strong boil, and boil for 10 seconds. Pour the caramel over the pears in the dish. Cool, and cover with plastic wrap. The caramel cream mixture will thicken as it cools. If it gets too thick, add about 1 tablespoon of water.

5. Arrange half a pear on each of four dessert plates. Add the pear brandy, if desired, to the sauce, and stir until the sauce is smooth and velvety. Coat the pears with the sauce, sprinkle the pistachios on top, and serve as is or with a few cookies or a slice of brioche, if desired.

PEARS IN GRENADINE

The time required to cook pears varies dramatically, and this must be taken into account when preparing this and other recipes. I use firm Bosc pears here, peeling and coring them before cooking, and, even though the cooking liquids boil up inside the pears in this preparation, it takes them 30 minutes to become tender. Well-ripened Anjou or Bartlett pears, on the other hand, will cook in as little as 2 or 3 minutes, while Seckels can take as long as 1 hour. ◠ Folded paper towels are placed on top of the pears in the pan to absorb some of the surrounding liquid and keep the pear tops moist, thus preventing them from discoloring as they cook. When cooked, the pears—saturated with the cooking juices—sink into the liquid. (See photograph, page 103.)

6   *medium Bosc pears (2 pounds)*
⅓   *cup lime juice*
⅓   *cup sugar*
⅓   *cup grenadine syrup*
1   *cup dry white wine*
1   *cup water*

1. Peel and core each pear from the base, leaving the stem attached and a little of the skin in place around the stem for decoration. Stand the pears upright in a saucepan that will hold them snugly in one layer, and add the lime juice, sugar, grenadine, white wine, and water. (The liquid should barely cover the pears.) Fold a length of paper towel in half and then in half again, and place it over the pears to cover their tops completely.

2. Bring the liquid to a boil over medium-to-high heat, then reduce the heat to low, cover, and boil the pears gently for about 30 minutes, or until they are very tender when pierced with the point of a sharp knife.

3. Set the pears off the heat, and let them cool in the pan for about 15 minutes, then lift them from the pan, and stand them upright in a serving dish. There should be about 2½ cups of cooking liquid remaining. Return the pan to the stove, and boil the liquid over high heat until it is reduced to about 1 cup of syrup.

4. Pour the syrup over the pears, cover, and refrigerate until cold. Serve one pear per person with some of the surrounding syrup.

YIELD
6 servings

TOTAL TIME
About 1 hour,
plus chilling time

———

NUTRITIONAL
ANALYSIS
PER SERVING
Calories 147
Protein 1 g
Carbohydrates 33 g
Fat 1 g
Saturated fat 0 g
Cholesterol 0 mg
Sodium 3 mg

PEARS AU GRATIN

It is important to use well-ripened pears for this dish, even if this means buying fruit that is slightly damaged or has darkened skin; the skin will be removed, and any spots on the flesh of the sliced pears will be concealed under the crumbs of the topping. ⬯ This is a nice way to use leftover French bread. You can substitute leftover cookies or cake, in which case eliminate the butter and sugar. Sour cream or whipped heavy cream makes a nice addition, but the dish is very good without either garnish.

YIELD

4 servings

TOTAL TIME

60 minutes

———

NUTRITIONAL
ANALYSIS
PER SERVING

Calories 312

Protein 3 g

Carbohydrates 49 g

Fat 13 g

Saturated fat 4 g

Cholesterol 16 mg

Sodium 130 mg

3   *very ripe pears (about 1½ pounds),
    peeled, halved lengthwise, and cored*
3   *ounces day-old French-style bread*
2   *tablespoons unsalted butter*
¼   *cup sugar*
⅓   *cup pecan halves
    Sour cream or whipped heavy cream
    (optional)*

1. Preheat the oven to 375 degrees.

2. Cut the pears lengthwise into ¼-inch wedges, and place them in a mixing bowl.

3. Break the bread into the bowl of a food processor, and process it until coarsely chopped. Add the butter, sugar, and pecans. Process until the mixture is mealy. (You should have about 2 cups.) Toss with the pears in the mixing bowl, and transfer to a 6-cup gratin dish.

4. Bake for 30 minutes, or until the topping is nicely browned. Allow the dessert to cool slightly.

5. Serve the pears lukewarm, with a little sour cream or whipped heavy cream, if desired.

Left: Pears au Gratin (this page); right: Tender Pears in Caramel Sauce (see page 140).

PEARS IN ESPRESSO

I like to use espresso in this recipe, but any leftover brewed coffee will do. I think that Bosc pears, which take longer to cook than most, lend themselves especially well to this preparation, although you can use another variety instead. If you can obtain tiny Seckel pears in your area, they are also good in this dessert. Substitute 1½ pounds of the Seckels for the Bosc pears.

YIELD
4 servings

TOTAL TIME
45 to 50 minutes,
plus cooling time

———

**NUTRITIONAL
ANALYSIS
PER SERVING**
Calories 183
Protein 1 g
Carbohydrates 44 g
Fat 1 g
Saturated fat 0 g
Cholesterol 0 mg
Sodium 8 mg

4   Bosc pears (about 1½ pounds total)
2   cups espresso coffee
    About 2 cups water
⅓   cup light brown sugar
1   teaspoon grated lemon rind
2   tablespoons Kahlua or another
    coffee-flavored liqueur
4   cookies (optional)

1. Using a small round scoop or a sharp-edged metal measuring teaspoon, peel the pears, and core them from the base. Stand them upright in a saucepan that will hold them snugly. Add the coffee and enough of the water to cover the pears completely; then add the sugar. Bring the coffee mixture to a boil, reduce the heat to low, and boil gently for 30 to 35 minutes, or until the pears are tender.

2. Remove the pears from the liquid, and arrange them in a serving bowl. Boil the liquid until it is reduced to 1 cup, stir in the lemon rind, and pour the mixture over the pears. Cool.

3. Add the Kahlua to the cooled dish, and serve the pears cold, with cookies, if desired.

PEARS AND ROASTED NUTS

Mixed nuts in their shells are a favorite dessert at my house in the winter. The flavor of roasted nuts is much more intense than that of unroasted nuts, and this freshly roasted flavor is preserved as long as the nuts remain in their shells. We crack the nuts right at the table and consume them with raw pears.

3   cups unshelled mixed nuts (walnuts, pecans, hazelnuts, and almonds)
4   small ripe Anjou or Bosc pears (5 to 6 ounces each)

1. Preheat the oven to 375 degrees.

2. Spread the nuts on a cookie sheet, and roast them in the oven for 20 minutes. Let them cool for at least 30 minutes.

3. At serving time, crack the shells a little, if you wish, arrange the nuts in a basket, and place them in the center of the table with a nutcracker.

4. Either peel the pears or leave them unpeeled, then cut them in half lengthwise, and, if you desire, core and quarter them. Crack open some of the nuts, and eat the pear pieces and nuts together.

YIELD
4 servings

TOTAL TIME
About 30 minutes, plus cooling time

———

NUTRITIONAL ANALYSIS PER SERVING
Calories 264
Protein 5 g
Carbohydrates 29 g
Fat 17 g
Saturated fat 1 g
Cholesterol 0 mg
Sodium 1 mg

ROASTED AND CARAMELIZED PEARS

⌒

The success of desserts with pears depends largely on the quality and ripeness of the fruit. For this recipe, Anjou or Bartlett pears are roasted at a high temperature in the oven for more than an hour, until their juice caramelizes and turns a rich mahogany color. The juice then is diluted with a little Madeira wine and served with the pears at room temperature.

YIELD

4 servings

TOTAL TIME

About 1½ hours
plus cooling time

———

**NUTRITIONAL
ANALYSIS
PER SERVING**

Calories 216

Protein 1 g

Carbohydrates 43 g

Fat 5 g

Saturated fat 2 g

Cholesterol 12 mg

Sodium 1 mg

4   *Anjou or Bartlett pears with stems
     (about 2 pounds), all equally ripe*
2   *teaspoons unsalted butter*
1   *tablespoon lemon juice*
¼   *cup sugar*
3   *tablespoons Madeira
     Mint leaves, for decoration*

1. Preheat the oven to 425 degrees.

2. Do not remove the stems from the pears, but peel them with a vegetable peeler. Then, using a melon baller, citrus spoon, or half-teaspoon measuring spoon, core each pear from the base.

3. Melt the butter in a small gratin dish. Stir in the lemon juice. Roll the pears in this mixture, and sprinkle them with the sugar.

4. Stand the pears upright in the gratin dish, and place them in the oven. Roast the pears, basting them with the emerging cooking juice every 15 to 20 minutes until they are nicely browned and tender when pierced with the point of a knife (about 1¼ hours). The juice should be caramelized and a rich brown color at the end; if it should begin to burn, immediately add 3 to 4 tablespoons of water to the gratin dish.

5. When the pears are tender, remove them from the oven. Add the Madeira to the dish, and carefully stir well to combine it with the juice.

6. Cool the pears to room temperature, and serve, spooning the accumulated juice over and around them. Decorate each serving with mint leaves.

Roasted and Caramelized Pears (this page).

PEARS IN CHOCOLATE

In this easy, flavorful recipe, pears are cooked simply with sugar, water, and vanilla. Then, when they are tender, cocoa powder and bittersweet chocolate are added to the cooking liquid to create a sauce.

YIELD

4 servings

TOTAL TIME

About 30 minutes, plus cooling time

———

NUTRITIONAL ANALYSIS PER SERVING

Calories 246

Protein 2 g

Carbohydrates 53 g

Fat 5 g

Saturated fat 3 g

Cholesterol 0 mg

Sodium 4 mg

4   *ripe Anjou pears (about 2 pounds), peeled, quartered, and cored*

¼   *cup sugar*

¾   *cup water*

½   *teaspoon pure vanilla extract*

2   *ounces bittersweet chocolate*

1   *tablespoon unsweetened cocoa powder*

4   *sprigs mint*

4   *cookies (optional)*

1. Place the pear quarters in a stainless steel saucepan, and add the sugar, water, and vanilla. Bring the mixture to a boil over high heat, then reduce the heat to low, cover, and cook the pears for 10 to 12 minutes, or until they are very tender when pierced with the point of a sharp knife.

2. Using a slotted spoon, transfer the pears to a bowl. (You should have about ½ cup of cooking liquid in the pan. If you have more, boil it to reduce it to ½ cup; if you have less, add water to bring it to ½ cup.) Add the bittersweet chocolate and the cocoa powder to the liquid in the pan. Mix with a whisk over low heat until the chocolate has melted and the mixture is smooth.

3. Transfer the chocolate mixture to a bowl, and cool it to room temperature. It will thicken to the consistency of syrup. (You should have 1 cup.)

4. Divide the sauce among four dessert plates, and arrange the pear pieces on top of the sauce. Decorate each serving with a sprig of mint, and serve, with a cookie, if desired.

BAKED PEARS WITH FIGS

Replace the figs with raisins, if you prefer, or bake the pears alone with the citrus juices, butter, and apricot preserves. This dessert should be made with fully ripened pears and served at room temperature.

2   ripe Anjou pears (about 1 pound total)
16 dried Black Mission figs (8 ounces total)
1   tablespoon orange juice
1   tablespoon lemon juice
¾   cup water
1   tablespoon unsalted butter, broken into pieces
1   tablespoon apricot preserves
½   cup sour cream (optional)

1. Preheat the oven to 400 degrees.

2. Peel, halve, and core the pears. Cut the figs crosswise into slices, and arrange them in a gratin dish. Place the pear halves, flat side down, on top of the figs, and sprinkle them with the orange and lemon juices. Then pour in the water, dot the pears with the butter, and spoon the preserves on top of them.

3. Bake the pears for 45 minutes, checking occasionally to ensure that the moisture doesn't cook away so that the pears burn; if necessary, add a couple of tablespoons of water.

4. Let the pears cool, and serve at room temperature, with some sour cream, if desired.

YIELD

4 servings

TOTAL TIME

About 1 hour, plus cooling time

———

NUTRITIONAL ANALYSIS PER SERVING

Calories 246
Protein 2 g
Carbohydrates 57 g
Fat 4 g
Saturated fat 2 g
Cholesterol 8 mg
Sodium 9 mg

PINEAPPLES

Most of the pineapples sold in the United States come from the Hawaiian Islands and are the Cayenne type. Contrary to common lore, the fruit is not necessarily ripe if the leaves from the center can be pulled out easily. One of the best indicators of ripeness is a sweet aroma at the stem end. Pineapples ripen very quickly in their last few days on the bush and almost double the amount of sugar they contain, so they are picked ripe. If picked unripe, they will not ripen further or increase their sugar content. ∽ Although pineapples are available year-round, they are best in the winter. They have relatively few calories; two slices, a reasonable portion, contain about 60. In addition to fiber, they have vitamins A and C. Pineapple juice contains an enzyme that is sometimes used to tenderize meat. ∽ Pineapple flesh is delicious raw in its own juice or with a little kirsch poured over it. You need to peel the fruit and remove the eyes and central core, which are tough and woody. Canned fruit is also good, and dried pineapple is available at most supermarkets. ∽ The pineapple has long been a symbol of hospitality, and sculptures of it are commonly hung over the main door in colonial homes.

The best pineapple I ever ate was in Puerto Rico; it was enormous, extremely sweet, and of the Red Spanish variety.

PINEAPPLE IN APRICOT SAUCE

Be sure to use a well-ripened pineapple for this delightful dessert. After the whole fruit is peeled and cut in an ornamental way, the bottom half is sliced horizontally and the slices arranged on a platter around the uncut top half, which is then decorated with a collar of strawberries. Served with a sauce made from apricot preserves, lime juice, kirsch, and mint, this dessert couldn't be more refreshing.

YIELD
4 to 6 servings

TOTAL TIME
20 minutes

NUTRITIONAL ANALYSIS PER SERVING (6 SERVINGS)
Calories 245
Protein 1 g
Carbohydrates 61 g
Fat 1 g
Saturated fat 0 g
Cholesterol 0 mg
Sodium 34 mg

1   *very ripe pineapple, with top and leaves intact (about 4 pounds)*
6   *strawberries*

APRICOT SAUCE

1   *cup apricot preserves*
2   *tablespoons lime juice*
2   *tablespoons kirsch or water*
2   *tablespoons shredded mint leaves*

1. Using a sharp knife, remove a thin layer of skin from the surface of the pineapple to expose the flesh. (The eyes will still be visible.) Then, still using the sharp knife, cut V-shaped diagonal furrows to remove the eyes of the pineapple and create a diagonal line design all around the fruit. Pull or cut off all the lower leaves from the stem of the pineapple, leaving only a few leaves at the top of the stem, for decorative effect.

2. Starting at the bottom, cut about half the pineapple crosswise into thin slices, and remove the core from the center of these slices. Place the top half of the pineapple, with stem and upper leaves intact, on a large decorative platter, and arrange the pineapple slices around it.

3. Using round toothpicks, attach the strawberries to the leafless base of the stem to create a decorative collar.

FOR THE APRICOT SAUCE
4. Mix all the sauce ingredients together in a small bowl.

5. Serve two slices of pineapple per person, with a strawberry from the stem, if desired, and a little sauce spooned over them. If you need additional pineapple slices, cut them from the bottom of the remaining pineapple half.

Pineapple in Apricot Sauce (this page).

SALPICON OF PINEAPPLE
(DICED PINEAPPLE)

⌒

Salpicon means "a mixture cut into dice," and this dessert consists of diced ripe pineapple seasoned with crème de cassis, cognac, and brown sugar. Ripeness is important here (see the introduction to Pineapple *Délice* on page 155). If you are fortunate enough to find a particularly sweet pineapple, reduce the amount of sugar. The dark raisins add color and a chewy texture that is appealing with the crisp pineapple.

YIELD

6 servings

TOTAL TIME

10 minutes,
plus chilling time

———

**NUTRITIONAL
ANALYSIS
PER SERVING**

Calories 198

Protein 1 g

Carbohydrates 25 g

Fat 1 g

Saturated fat 0 g

Cholesterol 0 mg

Sodium 4 mg

1   *ripe pineapple (3 pounds)*
¼   *cup crème de cassis*
2   *tablespoons cognac*
3   *tablespoons light brown sugar*
1   *tablespoon dark raisins*

1. Trim the pineapple at both ends, and cut it lengthwise into quarters. Cut out the core. Cut each quarter in half lengthwise again, and remove the skin from the wedges of fruit. Cut each wedge crosswise into eight pieces.

2. In a bowl, combine the pineapple pieces with the crème de cassis, cognac, and brown sugar. Refrigerate until serving time.

3. Spoon into six dessert bowls, and sprinkle the raisins on top. Serve very cold.

PINEAPPLE *DÉLICE*

The quality of this dessert depends on the quality of the pineapple. If your pineapple is ripe and flavorful, this quick and easy preparation will be delicious; if it's not, the dessert is not worth making. Opinions differ about how to judge pineapple ripeness. Some people insist that, if you can pull out a leaf from the crown of a pineapple, the fruit is ripe. I think you should rely on your nose. A ripe pineapple will have a pleasant, fruity smell.

½	teaspoon grated lime peel
1½	tablespoons lime juice
2	tablespoons honey
2	tablespoons kirsch
1	small ripe pineapple (about 2¼ pounds), leaves removed
4	slices pound cake or cookies (optional)

1. Mix the grated lime peel, lime juice, honey, and kirsch together in a large bowl.

2. Peel the pineapple, removing the skin and most of the eyes on the surface of the flesh. Stand the pineapple upright, and begin cutting it vertically into ¼-inch slices, stopping when you get to the tough core, turning it 90 degrees, and cutting again, until you have rotated the pineapple 360 degrees on its base and removed all the flesh. Stack the slices, and cut them crosswise into 1½-inch-wide strips.

3. Add the pineapple strips to the bowl containing the other ingredients, and mix well. Allow the pineapple to macerate in the lime juice mixture for at least 1 hour.

4. Spoon the pineapple strips and marinade into four bowls, and serve with slices of pound cake or cookies, if desired.

Pineapple Délice *(this page) served with Coconut Cookies (see page 214).*

YIELD

4 servings

TOTAL TIME

15 minutes,
plus marinating time

**NUTRITIONAL
ANALYSIS
PER SERVING**

Calories 115

Protein 1 g

Carbohydrates 27 g

Fat 1 g

Saturated fat 0 g

Cholesterol 0 mg

Sodium 2 mg

PINEAPPLE FINALE

Ripe is the key word here; if your pineapple isn't ripe, this dessert isn't worth making. Select fruit that is slightly soft to the touch and has a pleasant, fruity smell.

YIELD

4 servings

TOTAL TIME

15 minutes,
plus chilling time

**NUTRITIONAL
ANALYSIS
PER SERVING**

Calories 183

Protein 1 g

Carbohydrates 44 g

Fat 1 g

Saturated fat 0 gm

Cholesterol 0 mg

Sodium 3 mg

1   *ripe pineapple, with top and leaves
    intact (about 4 pounds)*
½   *cup orange juice*
2   *tablespoons honey*
2   *tablespoons pear brandy*

1. Make a crosswise cut about 1 inch below the top of the body of the pineapple. Reserve the pineapple top and leaves. Cut and discard a ½-inch slice from the bottom of the pineapple.

2. Place the pineapple on its side, push the sharp blade of a flexible knife into the flesh of the pineapple as close as possible to the outer edge of the flesh (where it meets the shell), and cut all around the flesh until you can remove intact a cylinder of pure pineapple flesh. Reserve the hollowed-out pineapple shell.

3. Cut the pineapple flesh crosswise into eight slices of about equal thickness, and, using a small round cookie cutter or sharp knife, remove the tough center or core (about 1¼ inches in diameter) from each slice.

4. Stack the slices in the order in which they were cut, and place them back in the shell. Set the reassembled pineapple in a glass serving bowl.

5. Mix the orange juice, honey, and brandy together in a small bowl, and pour the mixture over the pineapple. Refrigerate the dessert, covered, until serving time. (The recipe can be completed to this point up to 8 hours ahead.)

6. At serving time, place the reserved pineapple top with its leaves on top of the reassembled pineapple, and bring the dessert to the table. Serve two slices of pineapple per person with some of the surrounding juice mixture.

PINEAPPLE IN CANTALOUPE SAUCE

Three fruits are represented here: pineapple and plum slices are served in a beautiful sauce created by processing the flesh of cantaloupe. This dish is best if made with only ripe, full-flavored fruit (see the introduction to Pineapple *Délice* on page 155). The cantaloupe sauce can be used as a marinade for other fruits if ripe pineapple and plums are not available. Good substitutes would be watermelon, honeydew melon, and apples.

About ½ of a ripe cantaloupe (1 pound)
3   *tablespoons honey*
2   *tablespoons Grand Marnier liqueur*
    About ⅓ of a ripe pineapple, cut as a lengthwise wedge (1 pound)
2   *ripe red Santa Rosa plums (about 6 ounces total)*

1. Remove the rind and seeds from the cantaloupe, and cut the flesh into 1-inch pieces. (You should have about 2 cups.) Place the pieces in the bowl of a food processor with the honey, and process until smooth. Pour the puree into a bowl, and stir in the Grand Marnier. Cover, and refrigerate until ready to serve. (You should have about 1½ cups.)

2. Remove the skin and core from the pineapple, and cut the flesh crosswise into slices ⅛ inch thick. (You should have about twenty slices.)

3. Cut the plums in half crosswise, and remove the pits. Place the plums cut side down, and cut the flesh into slices ⅛ inch thick. You should have about twenty slices.

4. At serving time, divide the cantaloupe sauce among four dessert plates. Arrange four or five slices of pineapple on top of the sauce on each plate, and place one plum slice on top of each serving of pineapple. Arrange the remaining plum slices around the periphery of each plate to create a decorative border. Serve.

YIELD
4 servings

TOTAL TIME
About 30 minutes

———

NUTRITIONAL ANALYSIS PER SERVING
Calories 470
Protein 6 g
Carbohydrates 111 g
Fat 4 g
Saturated fat 0 g
Cholesterol 0 mg
Sodium 6 mg

PLUMS

Plums have been grown for over two thousand years, and there are hundreds of varieties. More than 75 percent of the plums consumed in the world come from California. The most reliable is the fleshy and juicy Santa Rosa plum, which has dark-purple skin, deep yellow-red flesh, and a very small pit. Other common varieties are the Queen Anne, which is quite large, with light-yellow flesh and mahogany skin, and the Mariposa, which has very red flesh and is good poached. The large, dark, and meaty damson is less common nowadays. ⌁ I remember with great pleasure the tiny, very yellow, very ripe Mirabelle plums that we ate right off the tree in France. These succulent fruits, about the size of a large cherry, are used in tarts and to make a brandy of the same name. Prune plums, the football-shaped dark-blue variety, which are dried to make prunes, are often called Italian plums in our local market and *quetsches* in France. With tiny pits and a somewhat green flesh, they are about the best for tarts. ⌁ The peak season for plums in the United States is May to October, although they are available from other parts of the world most of the year. Plums are quite high in vitamins A and C and potassium, and the calorie count for two of medium size is about 80.

Available in colors from deep yellow to deep blue, green, red, and purple, and in a variety of shapes, plums alone can be used to decorate a whole buffet.

POTTED PLUMS WITH PHYLLO DOUGH

I use plums here, but any fruit can be stewed in this way. Phyllo dough is available packaged in the frozen food section of most supermarkets. Conventionally, this thin dough is wrapped around fruit and the resulting packages baked. I find this process quite difficult; either the dough breaks and the fruit juice leaks through, or the juice makes the dough soggy underneath. Here, I gather each sheet of this tissuelike pastry into a loosely formed ball, perch it on top of the serving of fruit, and then bake the desserts until these pastry "hats" are brown and crisp. (See photograph, page 56.)

1   pound Santa Rosa plums (about 10)
2½ tablespoons unsalted butter
3   tablespoons shelled and skinned
    pistachio nuts
⅓   cup apricot preserves
1   tablespoon water
1   tablespoon (or less) sugar (optional)
4   sheets phyllo dough (14 by 18 inches
    each), kept wrapped until ready to use
    (to prevent dryness)
4   teaspoons sugar
    Sour cream or whipped heavy cream
    (optional)

1. Preheat the oven to 350 degrees.

2. Pit the plums, and cut each into four wedges (8 cups total).

3. Heat 1½ teaspoons of the butter in a saucepan. When it is hot, sauté the plums with the pistachios, preserves, and water, covered, over high heat for 5 minutes, or until the plums are soft. Remove the lid, and cook 2 to 3 minutes longer to reduce the remaining moisture in the pan. (The mixture should be thick, not watery.) Add as much as 1 tablespoon of the sugar to the plums if they are too tart. Spoon ½ to ⅔ cup of the plum mixture into each of four small (1-cup) ramekins.

4. Melt the remaining 2 tablespoons of butter. Unwrap the phyllo sheets, lay them out on a flat work surface, and, working quickly so that the paper-thin pastry doesn't dry out, brush the top surfaces of the sheets with the butter and sprinkle them with the 4 teaspoons of sugar.

5. Fold each sheet of phyllo in half, butter side out, and gather it gently into a loose tissuelike ball, taking care not to squeeze it. Place one ball on top of each ramekin, and arrange the ramekins on a tray. Bake for 25 to 30 minutes.

6. Serve the desserts lukewarm, with sour cream or whipped cream, if desired.

PLUM COBBLER

The old-fashioned dough topping for this classic dessert is quick and easy to make in a food processor. Assembly requires simply sprinkling the topping over pitted plums and baking the dish in a hot oven. Always reliable and good, this is one of my favorites.

DOUGH TOPPING

⅓ cup old-fashioned rolled oats
⅓ cup all-purpose flour
⅓ cup sugar
⅓ cup pecan halves
½ teaspoon ground cinnamon
3 tablespoons unsalted butter
1 tablespoon canola oil

1¼ pounds ripe plums (about 7) (Santa Rosa, Black Friar, or another variety)
⅓ cup sliced dried apricots
½ cup plain yogurt or sour cream (optional)

1. Preheat the oven to 400 degrees.

2. Place all the dough topping ingredients in the bowl of a food processor, and process the mixture for 15 to 20 seconds, just until it is crumbly.

3. Quarter the plums, and pit them. Place the plums in a 6-cup gratin dish, and distribute the apricots around them. Sprinkle the crumbly dough mixture on top.

4. Bake the cobbler for 40 minutes. Cool it to lukewarm, and serve with a rounded tablespoon of yogurt or sour cream, if desired, per serving.

YIELD
4 servings

TOTAL TIME
About 1 hour

NUTRITIONAL
ANALYSIS
PER SERVING
Calories 286
Protein 4 g
Carbohydrates 41 g
Fat 13 g
Saturated fat 4 g
Cholesterol 17 mg
Sodium 12 mg

QUICK PLUM AND ALMOND CAKE

This cake requires only a few seconds to process the flour and almonds together into a coarse powder, which is mixed quickly with the remaining cake ingredients. The batter can be cooked either in a round springform mold or in a loaf pan to make a type of pound cake. ⁀ If baked without the fruit garnish, the cake freezes well. (It is best not to freeze the fruit garnish, which would become soggy and mushy when the dessert was defrosted.) For best results, wrap the cake carefully in plastic wrap and aluminum foil before freezing it, and defrost it, still wrapped, in the refrigerator.

CAKE

1   cup all-purpose flour (5½ ounces)
1   cup whole almonds (5½ ounces)
⅔   cup sugar
1   teaspoon double-acting baking powder
1   teaspoon pure vanilla extract
½   stick unsalted butter (2 ounces), softened (with ¼ teaspoon reserved for buttering the mold)
2   tablespoons canola oil
2   eggs
⅓   cup milk

GARNISHES

6   ripe plums, preferably Black Friar or Santa Rosa (about 1¼ pounds)
3   tablespoons sugar
½   cup plum jam
1   tablespoon plum brandy or cognac

FOR THE CAKE

1. Preheat the oven to 350 degrees.

2. Place the flour, almonds, ⅔ cup of sugar, and baking powder in the bowl of a food processor, and process until the mixture is a coarse powder. Add the vanilla, butter (minus ¼ teaspoon), oil, and eggs, and process for a few seconds, or just until incorporated. Add the milk, and process for an additional few seconds, or until the mixture is smooth.

3. Use the reserved ¼ teaspoon of butter to coat the inside of a 10-inch springform mold. Pour in the batter. (It should be about ¾ inch thick.)

(CONTINUED)

YIELD

6 servings

TOTAL TIME

About 1 hour, plus cooling time

———

NUTRITIONAL ANALYSIS PER SERVING

Calories 581
Protein 9 g
Carbohydrates 79 g
Fat 27 g
Saturated fat 7 g
Cholesterol 93 mg
Sodium 219 mg

Quick Plum and Almond Cake (this page).

FOR THE GARNISHES

4. Using the point of a sharp knife, remove the pit from the stem hole of each plum. Rinse the whole pitted plums well in cold water. While the plums are still wet, roll them in the 3 tablespoons of sugar. Arrange the plums on top of the cake, spacing them evenly, and push them down into the batter until the bottom half of each is immersed.

5. Place the cake mold on a cookie sheet, and bake the cake in the center of the oven for 50 to 60 minutes, or until it is puffy and nicely browned on top. Cool the cake on a rack until it is lukewarm.

6. Mix the plum jam and brandy together in a small bowl, and brush the top of the lukewarm cake with the mixture. Remove the cake from the mold, and cut it into six wedges so that each serving contains one plum. Serve the cake while still lukewarm or just at room temperature.

PLUMS *AU SUCRE*

This simple dessert combines wedges of plum with lemon juice and sugar. The mixture is set aside to macerate, with an occasional stirring, for at least an hour, or several if you wish to assemble the dish well in advance. Serve the plums cool but not cold.

6 to 8 well-ripened Santa Rosa plums
(or another variety) (1 pound)
2 tablespoons lemon juice
¼ cup sugar
1 tablespoon plum brandy (Mirabelle or
Quetsche) or another fruit brandy, such
as pear or cherry (kirsch) (optional)
⅓ cup sour cream
Cookies (optional)

1. Wash the plums, and cut them in half. Discard the pits, and cut each half plum into thirds. Place the plum pieces in a bowl.

2. Add the lemon juice, sugar, and brandy, if desired, and mix well. Cover the bowl with plastic wrap, and refrigerate for at least 1 hour and as long as 6 hours, stirring the mixture occasionally.

3. Spoon the plums and surrounding juice into wine glasses or onto dessert plates, and serve with a dollop of sour cream and cookies, if desired.

YIELD
4 servings

TOTAL TIME
10 minutes,
plus at least 1 hour's
chilling time

**NUTRITIONAL
ANALYSIS
PER SERVING**
Calories 149
Protein 2 g
Carbohydrates 28 g
Fat 5 g
Saturated fat 3 g
Cholesterol 8 mg
Sodium 12 mg

RASPBERRIES

The raspberry may be the fruit most often used in professional kitchens. It is served fresh as a garnish to other fruits and desserts and is transformed into sauces, *coulis,* and sherbets. It is the most intensely flavored and delicious of the berries. ⌒ Whereas the strawberry wears its tiny seeds on the outside, the raspberry hides them inside, and, when the fruit is pureed for mousses, sherbets, sauces, or ice creams, it must be strained. ⌒

Raspberries are quite low in calories, about 60 per cup, very high in fiber if eaten with the seeds, and high in vitamins A and C. Avoid washing them, because they are very delicate and tend to get waterlogged. Since they are picked from bushes, they are usually quite clean. Mildew develops quite rapidly if raspberries are wet; spread them gently on a paper towel, and discard any that are mildewed. ⌒ Raspberries freeze quite well, and packaged, individually frozen, whole raspberries are one of my favorite purchases. Thawed berries are too mushy to serve on their own but excellent in sherbets, sauces, or mousses. ⌒ Although we commonly see dark red-blue raspberries, at the end of the season my market sometimes offers beautiful yellow raspberries, which are a golden color and have a sweet, delicate flavor. Raspberries are best when fully ripened on the bush. Regular raspberries are in most markets

Avoid raspberries frozen in syrup, because more than half of their content is sugar.

from the end of April until November, but their peak season is July and August. Berries

imported from other parts of the world are available in some markets most of the year. ➣

Raspberries can be served either raw or cooked. Cook whole berries gently and lightly, or

they will become mushy. If you are using them in tarts, be aware that they render a great

deal of juice, so add almond powder or flour to help absorb the excess.

PRICKLY MERINGUES
WITH RASPBERRY–ORANGE SAUCE

I give these individual meringues a distinctive look by pulling up on the surface of the egg white mixture to create "prickly" points on top. Meringues used to be served most often with a custard sauce made with cream and eggs. My intensely flavored fruit sauce, made with a puree of frozen raspberries mixed with preserves and diced orange, is a delicious, more healthful alternative.

MERINGUES

3   egg whites
½   cup sugar
1   teaspoon pure vanilla extract

RASPBERRY–ORANGE SAUCE

2   cups individually quick-frozen (IQF) raspberries, thawed
⅓   cup seedless raspberry preserves
1   large seedless orange (about 10 ounces)
12   mint leaves, shredded

FOR THE MERINGUES

1. Preheat the oven to 200 degrees.

2. Beat the egg whites until stiff but not dry. Add the sugar all at once, and beat for about 10 seconds more to incorporate it. Mix in the vanilla.

3. Line a baking tray with parchment paper. Using a spoon or a pastry bag fitted with a plain or fluted tip, drop or pipe four round or oval meringues onto the tray. Using a table knife or the pastry bag tip, pull up on the surface of the meringues to create prickly points. Bake the meringues for 3 hours, or until they are lightly browned and cooked throughout. Cool thoroughly, and store in an airtight container.

FOR THE RASPBERRY–ORANGE SAUCE

4. Push the berries and preserves through a food mill fitted with a very fine screen. Some seeds may go through; if so, strain the mixture through a sieve, if desired. (You will have about 1 cup.)

5. Peel the orange so that the flesh is totally exposed, and cut it into ½-inch pieces. (You should have about ¾ cup.) Add the orange pieces and the shredded mint to the raspberry mixture.

6. To serve, spoon some of the sauce onto each of four dessert plates, and place a meringue in the center of each plate. Serve immediately.

YIELD
4 servings

TOTAL TIME
About 3½ hours

NUTRITIONAL ANALYSIS PER SERVING
Calories 243
Protein 4 g
Carbohydrates 59 g
Fat 1 g
Saturated fat 0 g
Cholesterol 0 mg
Sodium 44 mg

CREAM OF RASPBERRIES AND YOGURT

This creamy fruit dessert looks much richer than it is. The berries are emulsified with the yogurt to create a smooth, luscious, but relatively low-calorie cream.

YIELD

4 servings

TOTAL TIME

10 minutes,
plus chilling time

———

**NUTRITIONAL
ANALYSIS
PER SERVING**

Calories 105

Protein 2 g

Carbohydrates 22 g

Fat 2 g

Saturated fat 1 g

Cholesterol 6 mg

Sodium 20 mg

2   *pints ripe raspberries (4 cups)*
¾   *cup plain yogurt*
¼   *cup sugar*
4   *strips lemon or lime peel or sprigs mint*

1. Place about a third of the berries, including any that are less perfect (damaged, wilted, or soft) in the bowl of a food processor with the yogurt and sugar. Process until pureed, then push the puree through a sieve or food mill fitted with a fine screen to remove the small raspberry seeds from the mixture.

2. Combine the remaining berries with the raspberry–yogurt sauce, and refrigerate until serving time (as long as 6 hours). Divide among four dessert dishes, and serve, garnished with the mint or peppermint.

VARIATION

Do not combine the berries and sauce in step 2. At serving time, divide the sauce among four dessert plates, and mound the remaining berries in the center of each. Top each serving with a strip of lemon or lime peel or a sprig of mint, and serve.

Left: Cream of Raspberries and Yogurt (this page); right: Raspberry Velvet (see page 172).

RASPBERRY VELVET

I often use individually quick-frozen (IQF) berries. Available year-round at most supermarkets, they are generally berries of high quality that have been picked and frozen (without sugar) at the peak of ripeness. Of course, if you have access to fresh raspberries, by all means use them. Here the berries are liquefied and strained first, and then the mixture is partially frozen. The resulting slush is served in sugar-rimmed glasses. If you prepare the dessert ahead and freeze the mixture until hard, be sure to defrost it under refrigeration for an hour or so before serving, to achieve the desired slushy consistency.

(See photograph, page 171.)

YIELD
4 servings

TOTAL TIME
About 15 minutes,
plus freezing time

———

**NUTRITIONAL
ANALYSIS
PER SERVING**
Calories 124
Protein 1 g
Carbohydrates 32 g
Fat 1 g
Saturated fat 0 g
Cholesterol 0 mg
Sodium 11 mg

1   *package (12 ounces) unsweetened
    IQF raspberries, defrosted, or about
    12 ounces fresh raspberries*
⅓   *cup seedless black raspberry preserves*
¼   *cup water*
2   *teaspoons lime juice*
1   *tablespoon sugar*
4   *strips lime peel*

1. Push the raspberries through a food mill with the black raspberry preserves, then strain the mixture through a fine-mesh strainer set over a bowl, to eliminate any remaining seeds. Add the water, and mix well. (You will have about 2 cups.)

2. Place the bowl containing the berry mixture in the freezer, and stir it occasionally until it is half frozen and slushy in consistency.

3. Meanwhile, place the lime juice in one small saucer and the sugar in another. Dip the rims of four stemmed glasses (preferably tulip champagne glasses) first into the lime juice and then into the sugar, to create a border. Place the glasses in the freezer or refrigerator until serving time.

4. At serving time, divide the raspberry velvet among the prepared glasses, and decorate each dessert with a strip of lime peel. Serve immediately.

RASPBERRY *GRANITÉ*

This *granité* can be made with fresh raspberries or with unsweetened frozen raspberries. Raspberry preserves intensify the taste of the berries and sweeten the mixture. The resulting puree is frozen, then lightly emulsified in a food processor and frozen again. The dessert is best served when hard enough so that you can scoop it out to form a large "curl." Especially attractive in champagne glasses, this refreshing sherbet is served with a little raspberry brandy and garnished with mint sprigs. It makes a perfect finish to an elegant meal.

¾ *pound fresh raspberries or 1 package (12 ounces) individually quick-frozen (IQF) unsweetened raspberries*
1 *cup raspberry preserves*
1 *tablespoon fresh lemon juice*
4 *teaspoons raspberry brandy*
4 *sprigs fresh mint, for garnish*
   Additional fresh raspberries, for garnish (optional)

1. Place the berries and preserves in the bowl of a food processor, and process until pureed. Strain through a fine strainer into a bowl. (You should have 2 cups.)

2. Add the lemon juice, and mix. Place the bowl in the freezer for about 2½ hours. The mixture should be hard-set but still soft enough in the center to be mixed.

3. Transfer the puree to the bowl of a food processor, and process for about 20 seconds. (It will "whiten" slightly.) Return the puree to a bowl, and place it back in the freezer for another 2½ to 3 hours.

4. To serve, scoop into glass dishes, and spoon 1 teaspoon of the raspberry brandy over each serving. Decorate with the fresh mint and a few of the fresh berries, if desired.

YIELD
4 servings

TOTAL TIME
15 minutes, plus 5 hours' freezing time

———

NUTRITIONAL ANALYSIS PER SERVING
Calories 250
Protein 1 g
Carbohydrates 63 g
Fat 1 g
Saturated fat 0 g
Cholesterol 0 mg
Sodium 32 mg

WARM RASPBERRY GRATIN
WITH SOUR CREAM

This is a great dessert to make when unexpected guests appear. Although fresh raspberries can be used, of course, individually quick-frozen (IQF) berries, available year-round in most supermarkets, are an excellent choice here. The frozen berries should not be thawed; they go directly from the freezer to the oven without defrosting. A Danish pastry, or, if you're in a bind, three slices of regular bread, can be used in the topping.

2   *large or 3 small day-old croissants (about 3 ounces), or a 3-ounce piece of slightly stale pound cake, or a large muffin*

2   *tablespoons unsalted butter, softened*

⅓   *cup sugar (less if using a sweet cake or muffin)*

1   *package (12 ounces) unsweetened IQF raspberries*

½   *cup sour cream*

4   *sprigs mint leaves, for garnish (optional)*

1. Preheat the oven to 400 degrees.

2. Break the croissants, cake, or muffin into pieces, and place them in the bowl of a food processor with the butter and sugar. Process, pulsing the machine for about 20 seconds, to chop coarsely and combine the ingredients. (You should have about 1¾ to 2 cups.)

3. Spread the frozen berries in a gratin dish deep enough so that the berries are about two layers thick. Sprinkle the topping mixture evenly over the berries.

4. Place the gratin dish on a tray, and bake the dessert for 20 to 25 minutes, or until the berries are very soft and the crumbs on top nicely browned. Cool to lukewarm. Garnish each serving with a generous spoonful of sour cream and, if desired, a mint sprig.

YIELD

4 servings

TOTAL TIME

About 30 minutes

NUTRITIONAL ANALYSIS PER SERVING

Calories 300

Protein 3 g

Carbohydrates 35 g

Fat 17 g

Saturated fat 10 g

Cholesterol 53 mg

Sodium 124 mg

Warm Raspberry Gratin with Sour Cream (this page).

RASPBERRY TRIFLE WITH NECTARINE SAUCE

Fresh raspberries are the centerpiece of this trifle, which also includes pound cake moistened and flavored with a little coffee extract. I use homemade yogurt cheese in place of the fresh cream traditionally found in this classic dessert, thus dropping the calorie count substantially. The cheese is made by draining nonfat plain yogurt in a strainer for at least 12 hours, to remove the liquid whey.　⌒　When considering the use of nonfat yogurt as an alternative ingredient in recipes, compare the following figures: 1 cup of nonfat yogurt contains 120 calories; 1 cup of sour cream contains 490 calories; 1 cup of heavy cream contains 830 calories; and 1 cup of mayonnaise contains 1,580 calories.

YIELD

4 servings

TOTAL TIME

About 20 minutes, plus at least 12 hours to make yogurt cheese

———

NUTRITIONAL ANALYSIS PER SERVING

Calories 257

Protein 4 g

Carbohydrates 46 g

Fat 6 g

Saturated fat 3 g

Cholesterol 63 mg

Sodium 139 mg

1　*pint nonfat plain yogurt*

4　*ounces pound cake, homemade or store-bought*

¼　*cup coffee extract (the first ¼ cup from a pot of drip coffee)*

8　*ounces fresh raspberries*

NECTARINE SAUCE

⅓　*cup peach preserves*

3　*tablespoons orange juice*

1　*nectarine (8 ounces), pitted and cut into ¼-inch pieces (1 cup)*

1　*tablespoon cognac*

4　*small sprigs mint, for decoration*

1. Place the yogurt in a strainer lined with paper towels, and set it over a bowl. Cover the yogurt with plastic wrap, and refrigerate it for at least 12 hours or as long as 24. There will be about 1 cup of liquid whey in the bowl, which can be drunk or discarded, and about 1 cup (8 ounces) of yogurt cheese in the strainer. Set aside 6 tablespoons (4½ ounces) of the cheese for use in this recipe. Reserve the remainder of the cheese for another use.

2. Cut the pound cake into eight slices, each about ⅜ inch thick. Then, with a cookie cutter, cut the slices into rounds 2½ to 2¾ inches in diameter. Reserve the cake trimmings. Place a cake round in the bottom of each of four small (½-cup) soufflé molds about 2¾ inches in diameter.

3. Using a brush or teaspoon, moisten each round of cake with about 1 teaspoon of the coffee extract. Place about ¾ tablespoon of yogurt cheese on top of each round, and press about eight raspberries into the cheese. Coarsely crumble some of the reserved cake trimmings on top of the cheese, and moisten the trimmings with about 1 teaspoon of the remaining coffee extract. Place another ¾ tablespoon of cheese on top of the crumbs, and press another eight raspberries into the cheese. Top each dessert with another cake round, moisten the rounds with the remaining coffee extract, and press them into place. Cover tightly with plastic wrap, and refrigerate.

4. Place all the nectarine sauce ingredients in a bowl. Mix well, cover, and refrigerate. (The desserts can be prepared to this point up to 8 hours ahead.)

5. At serving time, run a knife around the inside edge of the soufflé molds, and unmold the trifles onto dessert plates. Coat with the nectarine sauce, and decorate each serving with a sprig of mint.

RASPBERRY COOKIE-DOUGH *GALETTE*

This *galette* is made with *pâte sucrée,* or cookie dough, which produces a delicate and buttery crust that keeps well enough to last 4 to 5 hours on a buffet table before softening. Conventionally, the dough is cooked ahead, and then raw berries or poached fruits are arranged on top not long before the *galette* is served. The crust is sometimes lined with a pastry cream before the fruit is added, and often the fruit is finished with a glaze. For this recipe, the "less perfect" berries are combined with raspberry preserves and spread over the cooked shell before the nicest berries are arranged on top.

YIELD

6 to 8 servings

TOTAL TIME

About 2 hours

———

NUTRITIONAL ANALYSIS PER SERVING (8 SERVINGS)

Calories 505

Protein 5 g

Carbohydrates 69 g

Fat 25 g

Saturated fat 15 g

Cholesterol 93 mg

Sodium 254 mg

COOKIE DOUGH

2　cups all-purpose flour (10 to 10½ ounces)

1⅓ sticks unsalted butter (5 ounces), softened

3　tablespoons confectioners' sugar

1　egg yolk

1½ tablespoons water

FILLING AND GLAZE

4　cups fresh raspberries

1　cup seedless raspberry preserves

1　tablespoon raspberry brandy

FOR THE COOKIE DOUGH

1. Preheat the oven to 375 degrees.

2. Place the flour, butter, and sugar in a bowl, and mix them together with a spoon or break them into pieces with your hands until they are coarsely mixed. In a small bowl, mix together the egg yolk and water, and add them to the flour mixture.

3. Gather the ingredients together and place them on a board or counter top. Then, using the technique known as *fraisage,* with the heel of your hand smear about 3 tablespoons of the dough forward at a time until all the ingredients are blended. The dough should be completely smooth and the same color throughout. Repeat this *fraisage* a second time to make sure the ingredients are well combined.

4. Place the dough in the center of a piece of plastic wrap about 14 inches square, and place another piece of plastic wrap the same size on top. Roll the dough out between the two pieces until it forms a circle about 14 inches in diameter. Peel off the top plastic wrap, invert the dough onto a cookie sheet, and peel off the remaining plastic wrap.

5. With your fingers, roll the edge of the dough inward on itself to create a border about ½ inch thick all around. Press on the border so that it is tapered at the top, and, using your thumb and index finger, pinch all around the edge to create a decorative border.

6. Bake the dough shell for about 30 minutes, until it is nicely browned and cooked through. (The recipe can be completed to this point up to 12 hours ahead.)

FOR THE FILLING AND GLAZE

7. Using any damaged or soft berries, mix about 1½ cups of the berries with 4 tablespoons of the preserves in a bowl. Not more than 2 hours ahead of serving, spread the mixture over the base of the baked *galette* shell. Arrange the remaining berries on top so that they cover the entire surface of the *galette*.

8. In a small bowl, mix together the remaining preserves (about ¾ cup) and the brandy. Using a spoon and a brush, coat the tops of the berries with the glaze mixture.

9. Cut the *galette* into wedges with a sharp knife. (It has a tendency to break when cut.) Serve immediately.

STRAWBERRIES AND RHUBARB

Strawberries are one of people's favorite fruits. I remember with great fondness the wild strawberries that my brother and I picked along a road in the French countryside. We always looked for the ones that grew under the leaves, in the shade, because they had a much better flavor than those in the sun. The tiny, football-shaped berries are available occasionally at fancy markets, although they are quite expensive and never as good as the ones I picked as a child. Regular strawberries are available year-round in markets, but their peak season is from the end of April to the beginning of July. ⤙ Like many berries, strawberries are time-consuming to pick and therefore expensive. Many farm markets let you pick your own (and eat a few along the way). Doing this, you can choose the best specimens, those with the deepest color and most fragrant aroma, and usually pay about half of market cost. When enormous berries are available, choose them carefully; those that are green near the leaves and at their tips will probably have an acidic flavor. If you need to wash strawberries, do so before they are hulled; otherwise the water will get inside and adversely affect their texture and flavor. ⤙ Strawberries are delicious not only raw but also cooked in pies, on their own or with rhubarb, and they make

While the strawberry is sometimes called the inside-out fruit because its seeds are on the outside, the seeds are so tiny that nobody minds eating them.

excellent jams and preserves. Strawberries also glaze beautifully, whether the glaze is chocolate, sugar, currant jam, or raspberry preserves. ⟡ Strawberries are high in fiber, contain vitamin C, and are low in calories, having about 45 per portion.

Rhubarb is sometimes called the "pie plant" because this fruit is used mostly in pies. The stalks I have in my garden are cherry red, but those available at the market, often grown in hothouses, are a bit paler. Choose ripe, red, plump, shiny stalks. There is no need to peel rhubarb, as it cooks and looks better unpeeled. Rhubarb is generally cooked, although Eskimos eat it raw. Originally from Russia, it is commonly found and used in all the countries of Europe. Some people use it to clean pots; apparently, the chemical properties of rhubarb, especially its leaves, make pans shine. ⟡ Rhubarb is at its peak from April to the end of June, although hothouse rhubarb can be found almost year-round. It is quite high in vitamin A and contains fiber.

If any leaves are still attached to rhubarb stalks, be sure to remove them; the leaves and roots are high in oxalic acid and quite poisonous.

GLAZED STRAWBERRIES

This stunningly beautiful dessert is best made when large, ripe, full-flavored berries—preferably with stems—are available. The berries are dipped in warm currant jelly, which hardens around them as it cools. If the glazed berries are to stand for a long time on a buffet table, you might want to add a little unflavored gelatin to the jelly to make it even more binding and resistant to melting. (See photograph, page 185.)

12 large strawberries with stems
1 jar (10 ounces) currant jelly
    A few sprigs basil or another herb,
    or edible flowers, for garnish
4 or 8 cookies (optional)

1. Chill a plate in the refrigerator.

2. Wash the berries, and dry them thoroughly with paper towels.

3. Place the currant jelly in a saucepan, and warm it over low heat until it has melted and is smooth.

4. Holding the berries by their stems, dip them one at a time in the currant jelly. When they are thoroughly coated, lift them out, and drain off any excess jelly by scraping the berries gently against the rim of the pan.

5. Place the glazed berries on the very cold plate, and refrigerate them until serving time.

6. At serving time, arrange three berries on each plate, and decorate with the basil, other herb, or flowers. Serve with the cookies, if desired.

YIELD
4 servings

TOTAL TIME
10 minutes

NUTRITIONAL
ANALYSIS
PER SERVING
Calories 113
Protein 0 g
Carbohydrates 29 g
Fat 0 g
Saturated fat 0 g
Cholesterol 0 mg
Sodium 7 mg

STRAWBERRIES IN THE SUN

～

This recipe produces whole berries that are almost candied in syrup. In a conventional strawberry jam, the sugar is almost equal in weight to the strawberries; in this recipe, half as much sugar by weight is used. ～ For the syrup, sugar and water are cooked together on top of the stove, and then the berries are added. The mixture is transferred to a roasting pan and placed in the sun for about three consecutive sunny days to "cook" the berries. The liquid evaporates slowly, and the berries swell in the syrup. ～ You can cook the berries instead in a very low oven, which will take up to 20 hours, depending on how much liquid you want around the berries and how thick you like it to be. Remember that the liquid will thicken substantially as it cools.

YIELD

6 to 8 servings
(three 12-ounce jars)

TOTAL TIME

About 30 minutes,
plus 3 days in the
sun or 20 hours
in an oven

———

NUTRITIONAL
ANALYSIS
PER SERVING
(8 SERVINGS)

Calories 376

Protein 1 g

Carbohydrates 96 g

Fat 1 g

Saturated fat 0 g

Cholesterol 0 mg

Sodium 2 mg

1½ pounds sugar (3¼ cups) (more if berries are not ripe)
1½ cups water
3 pounds small, ripe strawberries (1½ quarts), hulled
Toast or cookies (optional)

1. Combine the sugar and water in a large stainless steel saucepan. Bring the mixture to a boil, and boil it for 6 to 8 minutes, or until it reaches the soft-ball stage (240 degrees). Add the berries, cover, and cook them in the syrup for about 2 minutes. Shake the pan gently (instead of stirring), and set the pan aside, covered, off the heat for about 10 minutes. At this point, the berries will have rendered their liquid and be very limp.

2. Transfer the mixture to a roasting pan. (The berry mixture should be about ¾ to 1 inch thick in the pan.) Cover the pan with a window screen (to protect the mixture from insects), and place it in direct sun for 2 to 3 days, until the syrup is reduced to the desired thickness. If sun is not available, place the pan in a 175- to 180-degree oven for 15 to 20 hours, until the syrup is of the desired thickness. Pour the mixture into jars, and refrigerate until ready to use.

3. To serve, spoon 3 or 4 tablespoons of the preserves per serving into small dessert dishes, and serve as is or with a piece of toast or a cookie, if desired.

Left: Glazed Strawberries (see page 183); right: Strawberries in the Sun (this page), with toast and in jar.

Fraises au Soleil

Red Wine and Cassis Strawberries

In wine-growing regions, berries—particularly strawberries—are typically combined with the local wine, and sometimes with a liqueur, and served as a dessert. Here, I mix strawberries with a fruity red wine and black currant or blackberry liqueur and serve them in the classic way, spooned into wine goblets. If desired, you may top the desserts with a little sour cream, and serve them with cookies.

YIELD
4 servings

TOTAL TIME
10 minutes

———

NUTRITIONAL
ANALYSIS
PER SERVING
Calories 133
Protein 0 g
Carbohydrates 22 g
Fat 0 g
Saturated fat 0 g
Cholesterol 0 mg
Sodium 3 mg

3   cups ripe strawberries, hulled
3   tablespoons sugar
3   tablespoons cassis (black currant liqueur) or crème de mûres (blackberry liqueur)
¾   cup dry, fruity red wine
1   tablespoon shredded peppermint leaves
4   tablespoons sour cream (optional)
4   cookies (optional)

1. Quarter the berries, and place them in a bowl with the sugar, liqueur, wine, and mint. Mix well, and serve immediately, or refrigerate (for up to 8 hours) until serving time.

2. To serve, spoon the berries and marinade into wine goblets. If desired, top each dessert with a dollop of sour cream, and serve it with a cookie.

STRAWBERRY *CLAFOUTIS*

⌒

Strawberries are used here in a *clafoutis,* a type of thickened custard usually reserved for cherries (which can be substituted for the strawberries, as can other types of berries). I use a little cornstarch as a thickening, combining it with eggs, sugar, milk, vanilla, and the berries. Unlike a conventional *clafoutis,* which is usually cooked in a double boiler, this is baked in a gratin dish. It is best served at room temperature.

¼ *cup granulated sugar*
1½ *tablespoons cornstarch*
1½ *teaspoons pure vanilla extract*
2 *eggs*
1½ *cups milk*
1 *pint strawberries (about 14 ounces), hulled (about 12 ounces hulled)*
1 *teaspoon confectioners' sugar*

1. Preheat the oven to 350 degrees.

2. Mix the granulated sugar and cornstarch in a bowl. Add the vanilla and eggs, and mix well with a whisk for 30 to 40 seconds. Add the milk, and mix until it is incorporated.

3. Quarter the berries, and distribute them evenly in a 4-to-6-cup gratin dish.

4. Pour the egg mixture over the berries, and place the gratin dish on a cookie sheet. Bake for about 40 minutes, until just set. Cool to room temperature.

5. Sprinkle the confectioners' sugar on top of the *clafoutis,* and serve it at room temperature.

YIELD
4 servings

TOTAL TIME
45 minutes,
plus cooling time

———

NUTRITIONAL
ANALYSIS
PER SERVING
Calories 182
Protein 7 g
Carbohydrates 26 g
Fat 6 g
Saturated fat 3 g
Cholesterol 119 mg
Sodium 78 mg

STRAWBERRY BUTTERMILK SHORTCAKES

Homemade strawberry shortcake is a hit with just about everyone, and this very easy version is no exception. In the shortcakes, I use both baking powder and baking soda. Baking powder is a mixture of baking soda and cream of tartar (tartaric acid); I use baking soda in addition to balance the sourness and acidity of the buttermilk. It is important to mix the ingredients for the shortcakes lightly and quickly, combining them just enough so that they hold together. The shortcakes are served with a garnish of sour cream, although yogurt would make a good, lower-calorie substitute.

1   *pint strawberries*
½   *cup strawberry jam*

SHORTCAKES
½   *cup all-purpose flour*
½   *cup cake flour*
1   *teaspoon baking powder*
½   *teaspoon baking soda*
1½ *tablespoons sugar*
½   *teaspoon salt*
3   *tablespoons unsalted butter, softened*
⅓   *cup buttermilk*

½   *cup sour cream*
4   *sprigs mint, for garnish*

1. Hull the berries, and cut about ¼ inch from the stem end of each berry. (This part of the berry tends to be less sweet, especially if the berries are not completely ripe.) Reserve these trimmings for the sauce. (You should have about 1½ cups of trimmings.)

2. Cut the trimmed berries into wedges, and place them in a bowl. Transfer the trimmings to the bowl of a food processor. Add the jam to the berry trimmings, and process until smooth. Pour the sauce over the berries, toss well, and set aside in the refrigerator for at least 1 hour and as long as 6 hours.

(CONTINUED)

Strawberry Buttermilk Shortcakes (this page).

For the Shortcakes

3. Preheat the oven to 450 degrees.

4. In a bowl, combine the flours, baking powder, soda, sugar, and salt with the butter, mixing gently with a spoon for 30 seconds at most. (The mixture should not be completely smooth.) Add the buttermilk, and mix with a spoon just enough to combine the ingredients into a soft dough.

5. Invert the dough onto a nonstick cookie sheet, and cover it with a piece of plastic wrap. Press on the dough until you have extended it to a rectangle about ⅜ inch thick. Remove the plastic wrap and cut the dough into 2½-inch squares. Bake for 10 to 12 minutes. Remove to a rack, and cool.

6. At serving time, cut the shortcakes in half horizontally. Arrange the bottoms on four dessert dishes, and spoon the berry mixture on top. Cover with the shortcake tops, and garnish each dessert with sour cream and a sprig of mint. Serve.

PISTACHIO FLOATING ISLAND
WITH STRAWBERRY SAUCE

This elegant dessert must be made ahead so it can chill and set before being unmolded. I make the floating island in a loaf pan, but it can be made in a round pan, too. Except for the small amount of butter used to grease the baking pan, the dessert contains no fat and only about 280 calories per serving. The colorful, easy-to-make sauce combines two distinct flavors: strawberries and black currants.

FLOATING ISLAND

½ *teaspoon unsalted butter*
5 *large egg whites (¾ cup)*
½ *cup sugar*
⅓ *cup coarsely chopped pistachio nuts*
2 *large strawberries, hulled and cut into ¼-inch dice (⅓ cup)*

STRAWBERRY SAUCE

10 *ounces strawberries, hulled*
10 *ounces (half a 20-ounce jar) natural black currant preserves (with berries)*
2 *tablespoons crème de cassis (black currant liqueur)*
2 *tablespoons chopped pistachio nuts, for garnish*

FOR THE FLOATING ISLAND

1. Preheat the oven to 350 degrees.

2. Grease a 6-cup loaf pan with the butter. Beat the egg whites until stiff. Add the sugar all at once, and beat for a few seconds. Fold in the ⅓ cup of pistachios and the diced strawberries, and transfer the mixture to the loaf pan.

3. Place the pan in a larger vessel (a small roasting pan works well), and surround it with warm tap water. Bake for 30 minutes, then remove the pan from the water bath, and allow it to cool to room temperature on a rack. The dessert will deflate slightly. Cover it with plastic wrap, and refrigerate it for at least a few hours. (The recipe can be prepared to this point up to 1 day ahead.)

FOR THE STRAWBERRY SAUCE

4. Slice two or three of the strawberries to use as a garnish, and set them aside. Place the remaining strawberries and the preserves in the bowl of a food processor, and process until pureed. Add the crème de cassis.

5. At serving time, unmold the dessert onto a rectangular platter. Sprinkle the floating island with a little sauce, and decorate it with the reserved sliced berries and the 2 tablespoons of chopped pistachios. To serve, divide the remaining sauce among six dessert plates, and top each with a slice of floating island.

YIELD
6 servings

TOTAL TIME
About 1 hour, plus chilling time

NUTRITIONAL ANALYSIS PER SERVING
Calories 281
Protein 6 g
Carbohydrates 55 g
Fat 5 g
Saturated fat 1 g
Cholesterol 1 mg
Sodium 66 mg

RHUBARB AND BERRY NECTAR WITH MINT

This is one of my favorite desserts in full summer, when rhubarb is available and mint abounds in my garden. I like to use a deep, berry-flavored red wine in this preparation. I add cranberry juice as well, but you should feel free to substitute another type of juice. Likewise, instead of the strawberry jam, you might take this opportunity to use up all the dabs of various jams taking up space in your refrigerator.

6 to 8 sprigs fresh peppermint
1 pound rhubarb stalks (all leaves removed and discarded), cut into 2-inch pieces
½ cup red wine (Beaujolais or Syrah are good choices)
½ cup cranberry juice
6 ounces strawberry jam
2 tablespoons sugar
6 ounces blackberries, blueberries, or strawberries, hulled
½ cup sour cream
4 to 6 slices brioche or pound cake, or 8 to 12 cookies

1. Remove the stem tops with a few leaves attached from 4 to 6 of the mint sprigs, and set them aside for use as a garnish. Gather the remaining sprigs of mint into a bundle, and tie them together with kitchen twine. Place the mint in a saucepan (preferably stainless steel), and add the rhubarb, wine, juice, jam, and sugar.

2. Bring the mixture to a boil, cover, reduce the heat to low, and cook for about 8 minutes. Add the berries, bring the mixture back to a boil, and cook, covered, for 2 minutes, or until the mixture is somewhat soupy. (You should have about 8 cups.) Transfer the mixture to a bowl, and remove and discard the mint. Cool, cover, and refrigerate until serving time.

3. For each serving, arrange about 1 cup of the rhubarb and berry mixture in a deep plate. Place 1 rounded tablespoon of sour cream in the middle, and top with one of the reserved mint sprig tips. Serve with a slice of brioche or pound cake or a few cookies.

RHUBARB AND STRAWBERRY *COULIS*

This dessert unites rhubarb and strawberries, fruits that are especially good when cooked together, as they are here, into a *coulis,* or thick soup. Sweetened with a little sugar and some jam, the *coulis* is beautiful when served in deep plates with a spoonful of sour cream or, if you like, whipped cream on top and sliced pound cake or cookies on the side.

1½ pounds ripe rhubarb, trimmed of any leaves and root ends and cut into pieces 1 inch wide by 3 inches long (4 cups)
1 cup ripe strawberries, hulled and halved or quartered, depending on size
¾ cup jam (any type of berry or other fruit or a mixture)
¼ cup sugar
¼ cup water
½ cup sour cream or whipped heavy cream
8 cookies or 4 slices pound cake (optional)

1. Place the rhubarb, strawberries, jam, sugar, and water in a large stainless steel saucepan, and bring to a boil over high heat. Reduce the heat to medium, cover, and cook for 10 minutes, or until the fruit is well cooked. Cool to room temperature, and refrigerate until serving time.

2. Ladle into soup plates, and serve each topped with a rounded tablespoonful of sour cream (or, if you want a richer dessert, use whipped cream on top and a few cookies or a slice of pound cake alongside).

YIELD
4 servings

TOTAL TIME
20 minutes,
plus cooling time

———

NUTRITIONAL ANALYSIS PER SERVING
Calories 302
Protein 3 g
Carbohydrates 63 g
Fat 7 g
Saturated fat 4 g
Cholesterol 13 mg
Sodium 47 mg

MIXED FRUITS AND PRESERVES

Most fruits discussed in this book can also be used in combination with one another. The shapes, tastes, textures, and colors of fruits are so varied that combining them often produces delicious and beautiful desserts. Pineapple with blueberries or strawberries, oranges with bananas and blackberries, and pears with plums and cherries are examples of mixed fruit desserts. ✑ I also use a variety of fruit preserves and jams in my cooking. The one I use the most is apricot jam, and I make my own in full summer when I can find ripe apricots. I like to combine frozen berries, especially raspberries, with raspberry and strawberry preserves to make a sauce. The mixture has an intense flavor, which can be married with many different fruits to create great desserts. ✑ Citrus fruits, particularly lemons, are often used in fruit mixtures. The acidity of lemon juice complements berries and prevents white fruits, such as apples, pears, and bananas, from discoloring. Combined with sugar or honey, lemon or lime juice makes a great basic sauce to serve on most fresh diced fruit. ✑ Another source of flavor for desserts is fruit brandies. Whether pear brandy, plum brandy, raspberry brandy, or cognac (grape brandy), these intensely flavored liqueurs enhance many fruit desserts. ✑ The enormous variety of fruits available in markets is sometimes staggering. Take advantage of the fruits at their peak in your market, and remember that the riper the fruit, the better the result.

Desserts can be created from fresh fruits, dried fruits, or fruit preserves.

CRÈME PÂTISSIÈRE WITH WINTER FRUIT

This attractive and delicious dessert is essentially a tart without the dough. Although vanilla extract can be used instead of a vanilla bean, I like the taste and look of ground vanilla bean, which appears as little black flecks in the pastry cream. I conventionally use older (and so somewhat dry) vanilla beans for grinding. It is a good way of using them up, and they tend to create a finer-textured powder than soft, fresh beans.

YIELD

4 servings

TOTAL TIME

About 20 minutes, plus cooling time

NUTRITIONAL ANALYSIS PER SERVING

Calories 289

Protein 4 g

Carbohydrates 57 g

Fat 5 g

Saturated fat 2 g

Cholesterol 115 mg

Sodium 52 mg

PASTRY CREAM

1 *vanilla bean*
3 *tablespoons sugar*
1 *cup milk*
2 *egg yolks*
1½ *tablespoons cornstarch*

GARNISHES

1 *ripe mango (about 12 ounces)*
1 *kiwi (about 4 ounces)*
½ *cup apricot preserves*
2 *tablespoons Grand Marnier liqueur*
1 *tablespoon shelled unsalted pistachio nuts*
   Pound cake or cookies (optional)

FOR THE PASTRY CREAM

1. Break the vanilla bean into pieces, and place with the sugar in a spice grinder or mini-chop. Process until the mixture is reduced to a powder.

2. Bring the milk to a boil in a saucepan. Meanwhile, combine the vanilla mixture with the egg yolks in a bowl, and stir well with a whisk for about 1 minute. Add the cornstarch, and stir well again.

3. Pour the boiling milk on top of the vanilla mixture, incorporate it with the whisk, and then return the mixture to the saucepan. Bring to a boil, stirring constantly with the whisk, and boil for 10 seconds. Place the mixture in a bowl, cover with plastic wrap, and cool.

FOR THE GARNISHES

4. Peel the mango, and cut it into slices. Peel the kiwi, and cut it into slices. In a small bowl, mix the preserves with the Grand Marnier.

5. When the pastry cream is cold, spread it in a layer about 1 inch deep in a gratin dish or other attractive serving dish. Arrange the fruit slices on top in one decorative layer. Using a spoon, coat the fruit with the preserve mixture, and sprinkle the nuts on top.

6. Spoon the fruit and pastry cream onto individual dessert plates at the table, and serve as is or with a slice of pound cake or a few cookies, if desired.

Crème Pâtissière *with Winter Fruit (this page).*

OLD-FASHIONED RICE PUDDING
WITH DRIED FRUIT

The proportion of liquid to rice is quite high in this recipe, so you end up with a creamy, almost soupy, mixture that is not at all like the dense, pasty rice pudding you may have encountered as a child. I add dried fruit—raisins, apricots, figs, and apples—to my pudding, but you can eliminate any of these that are not to your liking. If you are counting calories, top the pudding with yogurt instead of sour cream, or serve it without any topping.

YIELD

4 servings

TOTAL TIME

45 minutes,
plus cooling time

**NUTRITIONAL
ANALYSIS
PER SERVING**

Calories 372

Protein 10 g

Carbohydrates 65 g

Fat 9 g

Saturated fat 5 g

Cholesterol 32 mg

Sodium 127 mg

4 cups whole or nonfat milk, plus additional milk, if needed

⅓ cup sugar

1½ teaspoons pure vanilla extract

½ cup long-grain white rice

1 teaspoon grated lemon rind

¾ cup diced (½-inch dice) dried fruits (raisins, apricots, figs, apples, or others)

¾ cup yogurt or sour cream (optional)

1. Bring the milk, sugar, and vanilla to a boil in a saucepan. Add the rice, mix well, and bring the mixture back to a boil. Cover, reduce the heat to very low, and simmer for about 40 minutes, or until the rice is very soft. (The mixture should still be soupy at this point; if it is not, stir in enough milk to make it so.)

2. Add the lemon rind and dried fruits to the pudding, mix, and set aside until it has cooled to room temperature.

3. Spoon into four dessert dishes. If desired, top each dessert with 1 or 2 tablespoons of yogurt or sour cream.

CHOCOLATE AND FRUIT NUT CUPS

These small "cups" are more a candy or petit four than a dessert. They are especially fun to make with children, who love to select their own assortment of fruits and nuts and press them into the soft chocolate. The result is beautiful and delicious, and if you can refrain from eating more than two of them, the calorie intake is not too frightening.

12 mini-size foil or paper cups (1½ inches in diameter by 1 inch deep)

4 ounces bittersweet chocolate

1 tablespoon sliced almonds

1 tablespoon pecan pieces

1 tablespoon pumpkin seeds

1 tablespoon golden raisins

1 tablespoon muscat raisins

1 large strawberry, cut into 12 wedges

3 mint leaves, cut into pieces

1. Arrange the foil or paper cups on a tray. Melt the chocolate in a double boiler or microwave oven. (You should have about ⅓ cup of melted chocolate.) Divide the chocolate among the twelve cups, filling the base of each with about ¼ inch of chocolate.

2. While the chocolate is still liquid, arrange the nuts, pumpkin seeds, raisins, strawberry wedges, and mint leaves on top, and press on them lightly to embed them partially in the chocolate. Refrigerate for about 1 hour, until hardened.

3. To serve, remove the foil or paper casings, arrange the chocolate cups on a plate, and pass for dessert.

YIELD
6 servings
(2 "cups" per serving)

TOTAL TIME
About 20 minutes,
plus 1 hour's
chilling time

NUTRITIONAL
ANALYSIS
PER SERVING
Calories 119
Protein 2 g
Carbohydrates 14 g
Fat 8 g
Saturated fat 4 g
Cholesterol 0 mg
Sodium 1 mg

CRÊPES À LA CONFITURE WITH BERRIES

As children, my brother and I would sit watching my mother prepare crêpes, and we would eat them as quickly as they came out of the pan—sometimes just with homemade jam, but often with jam and fresh fruit. I duplicate this taste treat for my daughter for breakfast from time to time. It is easily done in a few minutes and is always a winner!

CRÊPES
⅔ *cup all-purpose flour*
2 *large eggs*
½ *teaspoon sugar*
¾ *cup nonfat milk*
1 *tablespoon corn or canola oil*
    Additional oil for greasing skillet

FILLING AND GARNISHES
Jam or preserves of best quality: strawberry, apricot, quince, blackberry, plum, or the like
1½ *cups mixed fruit: blackberries, blueberries, raspberries, strawberries, cherries, or the like*
Mint leaves, for garnish

1. Combine the flour, eggs, sugar, and ¼ cup of the milk in a bowl. Mix with a whisk until smooth. (The mixture will be fairly thick.) Add the remaining milk and the 1 tablespoon of oil, and mix until smooth.

2. Lightly grease the bottom of an 8- or 9-inch nonstick skillet with a little oil, and heat the pan over medium-to-high heat. When it is hot, add about 3 tablespoons of the crêpe batter, and quickly tilt and move the skillet so that the batter coats the entire bottom of the pan. (Move quickly, or the batter will set before the bottom of the skillet is coated, and the crêpe will be thicker than desired.)

3. Cook for about 45 seconds on one side, turn, and cook for about 20 seconds on the other side. As you make the crêpes, stack them on a plate with the first-browned side down, so that when they are filled and folded this nicer side will be visible. The crêpes are best made and filled just before eating.

4. To fill, spread each crêpe with about 1 teaspoon of jam, alternating the jam flavors to have different colors and tastes. Fold each filled crêpe in half to enclose the filling, and then in half again. Arrange the crêpes on a large platter, and sprinkle the fresh fruit over the top. Garnish with the mint leaves, and serve immediately.

YIELD
4 servings
(16 crêpes)

TOTAL TIME
35 to 40 minutes

NUTRITIONAL ANALYSIS PER SERVING
Calories 314
Protein 8 g
Carbohydrates 44 g
Fat 13 g
Saturated fat 4 g
Cholesterol 107 mg
Sodium 59 mg

Crêpes à la Confiture *with Berries (this page).*

PHYLLO TART WITH FRUIT *SALPICON*

This dish consists of two recipes: one is for a flavored fruit mixture, the other for an unusual and interesting phyllo dough shell in which to serve the fruit. Phyllo dough, available frozen in most supermarkets, is rolled and cut into strips. Tossed with butter, oil, and sugar, the strips are patted lightly into a tart shell and baked. The shell can be baked ahead, and the fruit—which can be varied based on quality and market availability—also can be prepared several hours before serving.

YIELD

4 servings

TOTAL TIME

About 45 minutes

———

NUTRITIONAL
ANALYSIS
PER SERVING

Calories 271

Protein 3 g

Carbohydrates 50 g

Fat 8 g

Saturated fat 2 g

Cholesterol 8 mg

Sodium 116 mg

SALPICON

⅓ cup best possible quality apricot preserves
1½ tablespoons lemon juice
12 ounces large Damson or Burbank plums (about 3)
1 cup blueberries

PHYLLO TART

4 sheets (14 by 18 inches) thawed phyllo dough (about 3 ounces total)
1 tablespoon unsalted butter, melted
1 tablespoon canola oil
2 tablespoons sugar

4 small sprigs mint or strips of lemon zest, for garnish

FOR THE *SALPICON*

1. Mix the apricot preserves and lemon juice together in a bowl large enough to accommodate all the fruit. Peel the plums, if the skins are tough. Pit them, cut the flesh into ½-inch dice, and add to the preserve mixture. Add the blueberries, and mix well. Cover, and place in a cool place (not the refrigerator) until serving time.

FOR THE PHYLLO TART

2. Preheat the oven to 350 degrees.

3. Roll the sheets of phyllo dough together into a scroll 18 inches long, and cut them crosswise into ¼-inch strips. (You should have about 3 cups of shredded phyllo.)

4. Place the phyllo strips on a nonstick cookie sheet. Add the butter, oil, and sugar. Mix gently until all the strands of dough are coated. Gather up the strips and press them into an 8-inch tart pan or a tart ring set on a cookie sheet.

5. Bake the phyllo shell in the oven for 15 to 18 minutes, or until it is nicely browned and crisp. Cool it in the tart shell on a rack, and then transfer it to a serving platter.

6. At serving time, spoon the *salpicon* of fruit into the phyllo shell, decorate the dessert with the mint sprigs or lemon zest, and cut it into wedges at the table.

CREAMY RICE PUDDING WITH FRUIT SAUCE

I prefer this recipe prepared with a sweet Asian-type glutinous rice, but another regular white rice can be used as well. The starchiest of all rices, short-grained glutinous rice is very white and has a sticky consistency when cooked. Although used as an all-purpose rice in some Asian countries, it is known as "sweet" rice because in China and Japan, particularly, it is primarily made into snacks and sweets. It is available in Asian markets and in the ethnic food sections of some supermarkets.

RICE PUDDING

⅓ cup (about 3 ounces) Asian-type glutinous (sweet) rice or another rice (not converted)

½ teaspoon ground cinnamon

3 cups nonfat milk, plus a few tablespoons, if needed

2 tablespoons pure maple syrup

½ teaspoon pure vanilla extract

FRUIT SAUCE

½ cup sweet apple cider, less 1 tablespoon to mix with cornstarch (see below)

½ cup fruity red wine

2 tablespoons honey

1 cup seedless red grapes (about 5 ounces)

1 red plum (about 4 ounces), cut into ½-inch pieces (½ cup)

1 teaspoon cornstarch dissolved in 1 tablespoon cider (see above)

1 kiwi (about 4 ounces), peeled and cut into ½-inch dice (⅓ cup)

FOR THE RICE PUDDING

1. Preheat the oven to 350 degrees.

2. Combine the rice and cinnamon in a large ovenproof saucepan. Stir in the 3 cups of milk, and bring the mixture to a boil over medium-high heat, stirring occasionally to prevent the milk from scorching. Cover the pan, and place it in the oven for 40 minutes.

3. Remove the rice from the oven. The mixture will be very mushy at this point, with a lot of liquid around the rice. Add the maple syrup and vanilla, and mix them in lightly. Transfer the mixture to a bowl, and set it aside, covered, to cool. When it has cooled, refrigerate it.

(CONTINUED)

YIELD

4 servings

TOTAL TIME

About 1 hour, plus cooling time

NUTRITIONAL ANALYSIS PER SERVING

Calories 245

Protein 7 g

Carbohydrates 45 g

Fat 1 g

Saturated fat 0 g

Cholesterol 4 mg

Sodium 103 mg

FOR THE FRUIT SAUCE

4. Place the cider and wine in a clean saucepan, and bring the mixture to a boil over high heat. Add the honey, grapes, and plum pieces, and return the mixture to a boil. Cover the pan, reduce the heat to low, and boil gently for 5 minutes. Mix in the dissolved cornstarch, and remove the pan from the heat. Add the kiwi, and pour the sauce into a bowl. Cool completely, cover, and refrigerate.

5. Although the rice mixture will thicken in the refrigerator, it should still be soft. At serving time, if it has thickened so much that it mounds on a spoon, stir in the few more tablespoons of milk to thin it. Divide the cold pudding among four soup plates, and ladle the fruit sauce on top.

BERRIES *RAFRAÎCHIS*

Rafraîchir means "to refresh," which is what this beautiful summer berry dish does for those who consume it. I double the quantity of berries to have enough for Berry Jam, the recipe that follows.

YIELD

4 servings

TOTAL TIME

About 20 minutes, plus cooling time

———

NUTRITIONAL ANALYSIS PER SERVING

Calories 175

Protein 1 g

Carbohydrates 45 g

Fat 1 g

Saturated fat 0 g

Cholesterol 0 mg

Sodium 19 mg

1   *cup fruity red wine (such as Beaujolais)*
¼   *cup sugar*
1   *cup jam or preserves (cherry, strawberry, raspberry, apricot, or other, or a mixture)*
2   *sprigs mint, tied together with kitchen twine*
1   *pound strawberries, hulled and halved (4 cups)*
12   *ounces blueberries (2 cups)*
6   *ounces raspberries (1 cup)*
     Cake slices, sour cream, and mint sprigs, for garnish (optional)

1. Place the wine, sugar, jam, and tied mint in a large saucepan, and bring the mixture to a boil. Mix well. Add all the berries, and bring the mixture back to a boil over high heat, stirring and shaking the pan occasionally to mix the liquid with the fruit.

2. When the whole mixture is boiling (this will take about 5 minutes), cover the pan, reduce the heat to medium, and boil it gently for 1 minute. Transfer the mixture to a bowl, and cool it to room temperature. Remove and discard the mint. (You should have 5 cups of the berry mixture.)

3. To serve, spoon about ⅔ cup of the berry mixture onto each of four dessert plates. Serve, if desired, with cake and garnishes of sour cream and mint. (Refrigerate the remaining 2½ cups of berry mixture to serve the following day, or use it to make Berry Jam, the recipe that follows.)

BERRY JAM

I place the leftover mixture from Berries *Rafraîchis* (see page 204) in a low oven for a few hours and transform it into this delicious jam. As good spooned over ice cream as it is spread on toast, it will keep for weeks in the refrigerator.

2½ cups cooked berry mixture from Berries Rafraîchis *(see page 204)*

1. Preheat the oven to 200 degrees.

2. Pour the berry mixture into an ovenproof glass dish or stainless steel pan large enough so that the mixture is about 1 inch deep in the pan.

3. Place the pan in the oven, and bake for about 5 hours to evaporate the moisture and concentrate the flavor of the fruit.

4. Transfer the jam to a jar, cool, cover, and refrigerate. Use within one month. Serve as a topping for toast, ice cream, pancakes, or the like.

YIELD
1¾ cups

TOTAL TIME
About 5 hours

———

NUTRITIONAL
ANALYSIS PER
TABLESPOON
Calories 25
Protein 0 g
Carbohydrates 6 g
Fat 0 g
Saturated fat 0 g
Cholesterol 0 mg
Sodium 3 mg

TARTELETTES AUX FRUITS PANACHÉS

A minimum of flour and butter is used in the dough for these small, flavorful *fruits panachés,* or mixed fruit, tarts. Thin dough disks are baked with a topping of lightly sugared apricot and plum wedges until the pastry is crisp and the fruit soft.

YIELD

4 servings

TOTAL TIME

1¼ hours

NUTRITIONAL ANALYSIS PER SERVING

Calories 277

Protein 4 g

Carbohydrates 39 g

Fat 13 g

Saturated fat 6 g

Cholesterol 23 mg

Sodium 71 mg

TART DOUGH

⅔ *cup all-purpose flour, plus a little flour for use in rolling out dough*

3 *tablespoons cold unsalted butter, cut into 3 equal pieces*

1 *tablespoon canola oil*

½ *teaspoon sugar*

⅛ *teaspoon salt*

1 *tablespoon ice water, if needed*

TOPPING

4 *small ripe apricots (8 to 10 ounces)*

4 *small ripe dark plums (8 to 10 ounces)*

2 *tablespoons sugar*

FOR THE TART DOUGH

1. Preheat the oven to 400 degrees.

2. Place the flour, butter, oil, ½ teaspoon of sugar, and salt in the bowl of a food processor, and process for about 10 seconds. Feel the dough; if it is soft enough to gather together, remove it from the bowl, and form it into a ball. If it is still dry to the touch, add the ice water, and process for another 5 to 6 seconds before forming it into a ball. Refrigerate the dough, or roll it out immediately.

3. Lightly flour a flat work surface, and roll the ball of dough into a very thin round or oval, no more than ⅛ inch thick. Using a 5-inch-diameter round cutter, cut four disks, gathering up and rerolling the trimmings as required. Carefully transfer the disks to a large cookie sheet or jelly roll pan, leaving a few inches of space between them.

FOR THE TOPPING

4. Cut the apricots and plums into thin wedges, and arrange them, alternating the fruits, in a spiral on top of each dough disk. Sprinkle the fruit with the 2 tablespoons of sugar, and bake the *tartelettes* for 30 to 35 minutes, or until the fruit is soft and the dough cooked through and nicely browned. Some of the juice from the fruit will leak out onto the cookie sheet; before it hardens and makes the tarts stick to the sheet, lift the tarts with a broad spatula, and transfer them to a cooling rack or platter.

5. At serving time, place a *tartelette* on each of four dessert plates, and serve lukewarm or at room temperature.

Tartelettes aux Fruits Panachés *(this page).*

CRUNCHY HORNS WITH FRUIT

Molded cookies are the showpiece of this recipe. The soft cookie dough is literally brushed onto a very cold cookie sheet, so that it adheres on contact. This technique makes large, very thin cookies, which bake quickly. They can then be lifted off the sheet while still warm and pressed or formed into different shapes. If you allow the cookies to cool too long on the cookie sheet after they bake, they get brittle and break as you try to mold them; should this occur, return them to the oven for a minute or so to soften them slightly before attempting to mold them again. ⌐ I use dried as well as fresh fruit in the mix I serve with the cookies. Although this is a particularly nice combination of fruits, you can make substitutions based on your personal preferences and seasonal considerations.

YIELD

4 servings

TOTAL TIME

35 to 40 minutes

―――――

NUTRITIONAL
ANALYSIS
PER SERVING

Calories 299

Protein 3 g

Carbohydrates 62 g

Fat 7 g

Saturated fat 4 g

Cholesterol 16 mg

Sodium 21 mg

COOKIE HORNS

¼ stick unsalted butter (2 tablespoons), softened

¼ cup granulated sugar

½ teaspoon pure vanilla extract

1 egg white

2 tablespoons all-purpose flour

FRUIT MIX

8 ounces strawberries, hulled and cut into ½-inch pieces (1¾ cups)

4 dried figs, thinly sliced (⅔ cup)

2 bananas (about ¾ pound), peeled and cut into ½-inch pieces

2 tablespoons lemon juice

2 tablespoons granulated sugar

1 cup low-fat yogurt (optional)

1 teaspoon confectioners' sugar, for decoration

FOR THE COOKIE HORNS

1. Preheat the oven to 400 degrees.

2. Rub a nonstick cookie sheet with ½ teaspoon of the butter, and chill the sheet in the refrigerator. (If you have a particularly high-quality nonstick cookie sheet or can line the sheet with a nonstick baking mat, you may omit the butter.) Place the remaining butter and the ¼ cup of sugar in the bowl of a food processor, and process for 15 seconds. Add the vanilla, egg white, and flour, and process for another 10 seconds.

3. Using a pastry brush, spread the cookie mixture onto the cold cookie sheet, forming it into four very thin disks, each about 6 inches in diameter.

4. Bake the cookies for 8 to 10 minutes, or until nicely browned. Remove the sheet from the oven, and lift the disks one at a time from the sheet with a metal spatula. Roll them while still hot around a metal cone to create a horn, or press the cookies into ½-cup glass bowls to make "cups." (If the unformed cookies cool and become brittle, see the suggestions in the introduction on page 208.) Let the molded cookies cool, remove them carefully from their molds, and set them aside until serving time.

FOR THE FRUIT MIX

5. In a bowl, mix together the fruits, lemon juice, and 2 tablespoons of granulated sugar. Refrigerate until serving time.

6. At serving time, arrange the cookie horns on individual dessert plates with the open end of the horn in the center of each plate and the "tail" extending beyond the edge. Arrange the fruit mixture to create the illusion that it is spilling out of the horns. Alternatively, arrange the cookie cups on individual dessert plates, and fill them with the fruit.

7. Garnish with yogurt, if desired, spooning it on either side of the cookie horns or cups. Sprinkle the confectioners' sugar on the fruit, the cookies, and the plates. Serve.

Uncommon Fruits

The best coconut I ever had was in the Caribbean Islands. I particularly like the green (unripe) nuts, whose delicious flesh is still gelatinous, so that I can scrape it out with a spoon and eat it like pudding. At that stage, before the flesh becomes white and very hard, the coconut water too seems creamier and more flavorful than when the coconut ripens. Try to pick a heavy specimen and shake it; you should hear the liquid inside. Use grated fresh coconut instead of the dried version you find at the market. Although coconuts are available almost year-round, the peak times are late fall and winter. To paraphrase a well-known saying, a person who plants a coconut tree plants clothing, vessel, food, and drink, a habitation for himself, and a heritage for his children. Coconut is quite high in calories, about 110 per ounce of flesh. The coconut milk you buy in cans is actually made from coconut flesh, which is pressed into a milk. The liquid found inside the fruit is coconut water. Coconut is often used in Thai and other Asian cooking.

Guava has a delicious, fragrant taste that resembles strawberry and pineapple, and the flesh varies in color from almost white to a tawny red. A guava should be very ripe if you will eat it raw; the unripe fruit is extremely astringent and inedible. Excellent in jams, preserves, and sauces, the guava is a good source of vitamins A and C. You can buy a guava jelly or paste canned or packaged in most supermarkets.

Tangerines remind me of my childhood, especially around Christmas. I particularly recall eating a small, firm, flavorful variety known as a clementine, which usually came to France

I've eaten fresh guava in Hawaii and Florida, but the best I ever had was from Mexico.

from Algeria. The tangerine is sometimes called the "zipper skin" fruit, because most varieties can be peeled very easily. Technically, the tangerine is only one type of mandarin orange. Fresh mandarins taste better than the canned segments that are available at supermarkets and often served as garnishes in Chinese restaurants. Many markets stock tangerine juice, which is extremely sweet and fragrant and less acidic than orange juice. The tangelo, a cross between a tangerine and a grapefruit, is sometimes available in markets. Tangerines and mandarin oranges are usually available in late fall and throughout the winter.

The papaya, another exotic fruit, is available in markets year-round. In Hawaii and Puerto Rico, papayas can weigh up to 20 pounds. Those found in mainland American markets usually weigh about 1 pound. They can be peeled easily with a small knife or vegetable peeler. ⌐ When buying a papaya, look for one that is half green, half red. It should be smooth, without many bumps, and it should give slightly when pressed with a thumb. ⌐ The beautiful seeds inside look almost like enormous beluga caviar. Papaya seeds are actually edible and have a peppery taste; some cooks crush them for use as a garnish. Papayas are relatively low in calories, about 60 for half of a fruit, and a good source of vitamins A and C. Like pineapple juice, papaya juice is used to tenderize meat because it has a special enzyme when ripe. Papayas can be served plain with just a little sugar and some lemon juice or mixed with other fruits. In the islands, however, papaya is often served with meat or fish.

A green papaya may ripen somewhat at room temperature but will never get very sweet.

The pomegranate is called a *grenade* in French, and the explosive grenade took its name from the fruit. The beautiful red seeds of pomegranates are used to make grenadine, that deep red syrup essential to a Shirley Temple cocktail. My wife loves to crush the seeds and use them as a garnish or decoration on fruit desserts. Beware of pomegranate juice; like beet juice, it stains almost permanently. ᔅ Pomegranates are available mostly from December to February. Although those found in American markets usually come from Asia or the Mediterranean countries, I have eaten beautiful locally grown pomegranates in Phoenix. They are rich in potassium and fiber and low in calories.

I believe that quinces make the best fruit jelly of all those available in markets. Although not very well known, this fruit can usually be found in markets in the fall. ᔅ Buy quinces that are yellow and have smooth skin. They should be fragrant, and the color of the flesh should be white or ivory. They have to be peeled, and the flesh is quite hard, with an even harder core in the center. They are not really edible raw, although we did eat very ripe quinces raw when I was a child. As I recall, the taste was astringent, but the fruit had a wonderful aroma. ᔅ Quinces have a high pectin content, which is one reason they make good jams, jellies, and compotes. The best quince preparation I know is *cotignac,* a paste or jelly made in Orleans, France. ᔅ A quince has 50 to 60 calories in a 4-ounce portion and is high in vitamin C, potassium, and phosphorus.

The quince is related to the pear and the apple, and it is often cooked in meat tagines (stews) in North Africa.

COCONUT COOKIES

One of the pleasures of residing in or visiting a locale where coconuts are grown is to enjoy the "milk" and flesh of the unripe fruit. The liquid in a "green" coconut is thick and rich, and the flesh, which is soft like gelatin, can be enjoyed with a spoon. Ripe coconuts are available almost year-round in supermarkets throughout the United States, and it is fun to break one open occasionally just to eat the flesh or use it in recipes like this. (See photograph, page 155.)

YIELD
About 16 cookies

TOTAL TIME
40 to 45 minutes

―――――

**NUTRITIONAL
ANALYSIS
PER COOKIE**
Calories 45
Protein 0 g
Carbohydrates 10 g
Fat 0 g
Saturated fat 0 g
Cholesterol 0 mg
Sodium 4 mg

1   coconut (about 1½ pounds)
1   cup confectioners' sugar (5 ounces)
1   tablespoon all-purpose flour
1   egg white
2   teaspoons pure vanilla extract

1. Using a screwdriver, make a hole in one or two of the coconut "eyes," and pour out the liquid (about ½ cup), which is sweet and resembles watered-down milk. (Although I enjoy drinking it, some people feel it is too diuretic.) Using a hammer, hit the coconut on all sides to shatter the shell and loosen it from the flesh. When the coconut is broken into pieces, use a small paring knife to pry the flesh from the shell pieces. (Be sure to hold the pieces with a towel when prying out the flesh to protect your hands.) When you have removed the flesh, use a vegetable peeler or paring knife to remove the dark, tough, thin skin from the flesh, and cut the flesh into ½-inch pieces. (You will have 9 to 10 ounces of flesh, enough for two batches of cookies. If making only one batch, freeze the remaining 4 to 5 ounces of flesh for later use.)

2. Position an oven rack about a third of the way from top of the oven. Preheat the oven to 375 degrees.

3. Put half the coconut flesh (about 4½ ounces) into the bowl of a food processor, and process it until finely chopped. Add the sugar, flour, egg white, and vanilla, and process the mixture for about 10 seconds, or until it is well combined.

4. Line a large cookie sheet with a nonstick plastic baking sheet (or use a nonstick cookie sheet). Drop tablespoons of the cookie batter about 3 inches apart on the sheet. Bake in the upper third of the oven for about 15 minutes, or until the top surface of the cookies is evenly browned.

5. Remove the cookies from the cookie sheet while they are still hot, and cool them on a wire rack. When they are cold, store them in an airtight container.

GUAVA-PASTE TOASTS WITH MINT

This dish holds happy taste memories of childhood for my wife. Her Puerto Rican mother served guava paste often, and I have learned to like it too, especially in combination with a little cream cheese and mint. You'll find it in the ethnic food sections of most supermarkets and in Latin American specialty food stores. This preparation is good not only as a dessert but also as an afternoon snack or a buffet dish. The leftover guava paste, well wrapped, will keep for several weeks in the refrigerator. (See photograph, page 216.)

4   thin slices white bread, crust removed
1   can (1½ pounds) guava paste
4   ounces cream cheese
24 mint leaves

1. No more than 30 minutes before serving, toast the bread slices lightly, and cut each of them into six pieces.

2. On each piece, place a small cube or chunk or guava paste, and top it with a small slice of cream cheese. Garnish each toast with a mint leaf, and arrange the toasts on a plate. Serve as a dessert or snack.

YIELD
4 servings

TOTAL TIME
10 minutes

———

NUTRITIONAL
ANALYSIS
PER SERVING
Calories 308
Protein 4 g
Carbohydrates 48 g
Fat 11 g
Saturated fat 6 g
Cholesterol 32 mg
Sodium 222 mg

PAPAYA SEGMENTS WITH TANGERINE
SABAYON AND POMEGRANATE SEEDS

This dessert takes advantage of some uncommon and exotic fruits that are generally available during the winter months. It could be prepared with mango replacing the papaya and with orange juice instead of tangerine juice. If pomegranates are not available, decorate the dessert with sprigs of mint. ⌒ The *sabayon* sauce should be served warm. Since it may break down if made ahead and kept warm in a double boiler, it is preferable to make it no more than an hour before serving.

2   *small papayas (about 10 ounces each)*
½   *cup water*
2   *tablespoons sugar*
1   *pomegranate*

SABAYON SAUCE

2   *egg yolks*
3   *tablespoons sugar*
¼   *cup tangerine juice*
1   *tablespoon Grand Marnier liqueur*

1. Peel and halve the papayas, and cut the flesh into ½-inch wedges. Place the wedges in a skillet with the water and the 2 tablespoons of sugar. Bring the mixture to a boil, cover, reduce the heat to low, and cook for 5 minutes, or until the wedges are tender but still firm. Uncover, and cook over medium-to-high heat for 1 to 2 minutes, or until all the liquid has evaporated. Cover the skillet, and set aside.

2. Score the skin of the pomegranate all the way around with a knife, and pry the fruit open with your hands. Break each half in half again so you have four pieces. Grasp each piece so the seeded side of the pomegranate rests against your spread fingers, and hold your hand palm side up over a bowl of tap water. Using the rounded end of a wooden spoon, tap the skin side of the fruit vigorously to dislodge the seeds, and let them fall into the water in the bowl. (If any of the cottony membrane surrounding the seeds falls into the water, remove it from the surface, and discard it; the seeds, which are heavier, will sink to the bottom of the bowl.) Drain off the water in the bowl, and set the seeds aside.

(CONTINUED)

Left: Guava-Paste Toasts with Mint (see page 215); right: Papaya Segments with Tangerine Sabayon *and Pomegranate Seeds (this page).*

FOR THE *SABAYON* SAUCE

3. No more than 1 hour before serving time, place the egg yolks, 3 tablespoons of sugar, tangerine juice, and Grand Marnier in a bowl. Place the bowl in a skillet containing enough boiling water to immerse the bottom of the bowl, and set the skillet and bowl off the heat. Whisk the mixture for 4 to 5 minutes, or until it is has tripled in volume and is thick, foamy, and silky.

4. Divide the lukewarm wedges of papaya among four dessert plates, and coat them with the tangerine *sabayon*. Sprinkle the pomegranate seeds on top, and serve immediately.

QUINCE SOUFFLÉS WITH PEACH JAM SAUCE

I make this recipe in late autumn, when quinces are available and ripe. The soufflés can be made with pears or apples instead, although both of these fruits cook faster than quinces and will not hold their shape as well. The quince pieces could also be served as they are after step 2 of the recipe is completed. Browned and caramelized, they are good served cool with a bit of sour cream, if desired.

YIELD

4 servings

TOTAL TIME

About 1½ hours

————

NUTRITIONAL
ANALYSIS
PER SERVING

Calories 307

Protein 6 g

Carbohydrates 50 g

Fat 11 g

Saturated fat 6 g

Cholesterol 178 mg

Sodium 65 mg

2   quinces (about 1½ pounds)
1   tablespoon plus 4 teaspoons sugar
1   cup water
2   tablespoons plus 1 teaspoon
    unsalted butter
1   teaspoon pure vanilla extract
4   tablespoons lemon juice
1   tablespoon pear brandy (optional)
⅓   cup peach or apricot jam
3   large eggs, separated

1. Using a small paring knife or a vegetable peeler, peel the quinces. Then quarter them, core the quarters, and cut the flesh into 1-inch pieces.

2. Place the quince pieces in a skillet with 1 tablespoon of the sugar, the water, 2 tablespoons of the butter, the vanilla, and 2 tablespoons of the lemon juice. Bring the

mixture to a boil, cover, reduce the heat to low, and cook gently for 1 hour. (There should be very little moisture left.) Uncover, increase the heat to medium-high, and cook, turning the pieces of quince occasionally, for about 10 minutes, or until they are all nicely browned and caramelized. (You should have about 2 cups.)

3. Remove about half of the quince mixture from the pan, and place it in a bowl with the remaining 2 tablespoons of lemon juice, the pear brandy (if desired), and the jam. Mix well. Set this sauce aside to be served with the soufflés.

4. Using the remaining 1 teaspoon of butter, butter four small (¾-cup) ovenproof molds. Sprinkle 1 teaspoon of the remaining sugar in each mold, and shake it gently to distribute the sugar evenly on the bottom and sides. Refrigerate the molds.

5. Preheat the oven to 375 degrees.

6. Place the remaining quince mixture in the bowl of a food processor, and process it for about 10 seconds, or until it is pureed. Return the puree to a saucepan, and heat it (adding 1 or 2 tablespoons of water if the mixture is very thick), until it comes to a boil. Add the egg yolks, and mix well.

7. Beat the egg whites until they hold a soft peak but are not too firm. Using a rubber spatula, combine the beaten whites with the quince puree, and transfer the mixture to the prepared molds. (It should fill the molds.)

8. Arrange the molds on a cookie sheet, and bake them for 12 to 15 minutes. Meanwhile, divide the reserved quince-and-peach sauce among four dessert plates.

9. When the soufflés are cooked, unmold them, prying them a little with a knife or fork, if necessary. Place each soufflé on top of the sauce on a dessert place, and serve immediately.